Corporate Relationship Management Strategy

Corporate Relationship Management Strategy

Roxana D. Maiorescu

BUSINESS EXPERT PRESS
Leader in applied, concise business books

Corporate Relationship Management Strategy

Copyright © Business Expert Press, LLC, 2025

Cover design by Charlene Kronstedt

Interior design by Exeter Premedia Services Private Ltd., Chennai, India

First published in 2025 by
Business Expert Press, LLC
222 East 46th Street, New York, NY 10017
www.businessexpertpress.com

ISBN-13: 978-1-63742-756-9 (paperback)
ISBN-13: 978-1-63742-757-6 (e-book)

Business Expert Press Corporate Communication Collection

First edition: 2025

10 9 8 7 6 5 4 3 2 1

To my marvelous four-year-old Maeve, with the utmost conviction that her brilliance, curiosity, and inexhaustible energy will enable her to achieve anything she sets her mind to.
To Dan and Luminita Maiorescu, for setting the standard for intellectual engagement.

Description

This book is perfect for corporate leaders, marketing communication practitioners, and students who want to gain a deep understanding of effective relationship management.

It draws on research from business, organizational psychology, and communication, whose insights it applies to practice through clear and practical examples. The chapters discuss the process of building and maintaining relationships via the consistent implementation of corporate values to ensure the stakeholders' identification with the company.

The reader will explore relationship management with employees and consumers in local and international environments, in offline and online interactions, and in times of crises. Finally, the chapters represent a journey into the role that leadership styles, internal cultures, and social media play in relationship management.

Contents

Acknowledgments

I am thankful to Dr. Soumitro Sen, Dr. Agaptus Anaele, and Mr. Joe Harkin, whose insights into corporate relationship management shaped this book, its format, and its style.

Introduction

"Coming together is the beginning. Keeping together is progress. Working together a success." This insightful recognition represents one of Henry Ford's most famous quotes. Today, his words reverberate in the mission statement of the company he founded in 1903: Ford Motor Company, currently the second largest U.S.-based car manufacturer. Today, the values of the company, among which "Put People First," "Do the Right Thing," and "Create Tomorrow" accurately depict Henry Ford's vision and story of success.

Henry Ford "created tomorrow" by making the vehicle affordable to every American. In 1903, he built Model A and won the right to produce it by fighting in court against a virtual monopoly that had been considered impossible to defeat. He perfected the assembly line which, in turn, enabled him to standardize the eight-hour workday. Consequently, Ford Motor represented the first company whose employees did not spend days and oftentimes weeks away from their families in an attempt to finish up a product. Henry Ford's focus on "putting people first" and "doing the right thing" further materialized in 1914 when he decided to pay his employees double the wages offered by other companies. Soon corporate America felt compelled to adopt a similar compensation method, and employees across the country were finally making livable wages (Stanford 2023).

The continuity of Henry Ford's values was captured by his great-grandson, William Ford, executive chair of the company, who argued:

> Ford is a family company and we stand together even when times are tough. For 118 years, our values have driven us to do the right thing and be there for one another. (Our Ford Purpose 2023)

Throughout its history, the company lived up to its value of putting people first as it paused vehicle production to manufacture medical equipment in times of crises. For example, during the COVID-19 pandemic, Ford Motor Company produced around 50,000 ventilators that were distributed to hospitals across the United States that had found themselves in dire need of medical equipment. The production of ventilators constituted a continuation of Henry Ford's tradition of placing the vehicle production on hold in order to address an imperative. Specifically, in 1941, as rural America had been facing a crisis of premature births, Ford Motor switched from vehicle manufacturing to the production of incubators (Kluger 2020). Further, in the 1940s, when the United States was witnessing a rise in the number of children affected by polio, Henry Ford used his supplies of plastic and rubber to produce a medical device called the iron lung. The device prevented the death and paralysis of many children affected by polio (Kluger 2020).

Over Ford's 120 years of history, the consistent implementation of values in corporate operations and decision making enabled the company to establish a solid identity that made the brand recognizable around the world. From India to Germany, drivers who buy a Ford vehicle recognize the value of "creating tomorrow" in the innovative features of their cars. From Canada to Hungary, job applicants interview for a position with Ford knowing that they are about to become an intrinsic part of a goal that is greater than business.

Values form the identity of a company, and their consistent implementation across operations enables corporations to project what they stand for to both their internal stakeholders (employees) and their external public (shareholders, consumers, journalists, activists, and the government). Corporate identity is particularly important for attracting primary stakeholder groups, such as employees and consumers, whom companies depend on for survival and success. By interacting with a company that embeds its values in each of its operations, consumers and employees may perceive that, to some extent, some of its values converge with their own. Therefore, they are likely to identify with that company. Corporate communication professionals leverage this identification to establish and maintain relationships with stakeholders.

Identification has been shown in research to represent an asset for both companies and stakeholders. Namely, internally, corporate identification triggers employee motivation and loyalty, a positive internal culture, and enhanced creativity (Stojanović et al. 2020). Externally, identification leads to increased sales and consumer retention (Fernandez-Ferrin, Castro-González, and Bande 2021). For example, when choosing between two similarly priced cars, a driver may decide to buy a Ford Bronco over a Jeep Renegade if they have previously developed a relationship with Ford. It is equally important to note that employees and consumers who identify with a corporation are more likely to speak up and provide feedback. By doing so, they lead to the development and delivery of superior products and services. In addition, their input enables the company to avert crises, including recalls and accidents, and facilitates the adjustment to an ever-changing market.

The purpose of this book is to explore how companies develop successful relationships through the constant embedding of corporate values across several functions. Join me on a journey that applies research insights to practice and explores relationship management, corporate identity, and values in a variety of settings: internally and externally, online and offline, in local and global business environments.

Here is a preview of our journey:

The book is divided into three parts. Part 1 is dedicated to internal communication while Part 2 exposes the reader to relationship management with external stakeholder groups. Finally, in Part 3, the book details ways to assess relationship management by focusing on less known tools, whose effectiveness cannot be overstated.

Chapter 1 introduces the concept of corporate values, corporate identity, and corporate identification and highlights their role in the development of stakeholder relationships. Further, it discusses the use of storytelling and strategic ambiguity in triggering identification with a company. To illustrate these concepts, the chapter provides practical examples with respect to General Motors, the Kraft Heinz Company, and Kodak.

Chapter 2 tackles employee engagement and the way corporate values can be used to develop and maintain relationships across the employee base both face-to-face and on internal social media platforms. For this purpose, the chapter provides insights into how to establish and manage an internal online community centered around values. Undoubtedly, leaders exert tremendous influence over the development of successful employee relationships, the facilitation of corporate identification, and the internal culture. Chapter 3 explores the role of specific leadership and communication styles in accomplishing the preceding. Furthermore, the chapter applies several theoretical concepts to practice by providing examples from Microsoft and General Motors and by analyzing the leadership styles of the companies' CEOs.

When a corporation faces a crisis, employee morale is likely to be low, particularly as the company deals with an onslaught of negative media coverage. Corporate identification can determine whether the employees' response to the crisis will enable the company to recover quickly or, conversely, whether the employees will engage in negative word-of-mouth. The preceding is discussed in Chapter 4, which provides illustrations from Johnson & Johnson, Disney, and France Telecom. The next chapter revolves around happy employees whose enthusiasm is contagious. What better way to create happiness in the workplace than by fostering a positive internal culture? For this purpose, Chapter 5 discusses the role of relationship management, corporate values, and identity in triggering and maintaining a workplace atmosphere in which everyone feels supported and valued.

The topic of external relationship management is emphasized in Chapter 6, which details the way companies can leverage corporate identification to establish and maintain relationships with (potential) consumers, activist groups, the media, and the government. Theoretical concepts are supported with insight into Wendy's relationship management processes. Because business has gone more and more global and cultural competency represents the sine qua non for business success, Chapter 7 offers strategies for the adaptation of corporate values to international environments. It analyzes global relationship management at IKEA and Nike.

When corporations started to be placed under the magnifying glass for their operations and societal contributions, they often embraced corporate social responsibility (CSR) and, more recently, political activism, both of which are discussed in Chapter 8. The chapter deals with the role played by relationship management and corporate identification in determining the embracement of causes that benefit both society and companies. It discusses the cases of Patagonia and IBM. Further, Chapter 9 discusses crisis and scandal management by looking at Christian Dior and Toyota.

The coverage revolves around the difference between crises related to products, services, and operations on the one hand and scandals, or crises of morality, on the other hand. In addition, Chapter 9 emphasizes the role of social media in engendering crises and scandals and discusses how to prevent and address them. Finally, Chapter 10 exposes the reader to the assessment of corporate identification and relationship management in online and offline settings. It provides insight into qualitative methods of assessment, including ethnography, netnography, and autoethnography. I hope you will enjoy our journey into the fascinating world of applied research!

PART 1

Internal Communication

CHAPTER 1

Relationship Management and Corporate Identification

This chapter explores corporate values, corporate identity, and corporate identification and highlights their role in the development of stakeholder relationships. Further, it provides strategies through which values are strategically promoted to facilitate corporate identification, such as storytelling and strategic ambiguity. To illustrate these concepts, the chapter provides examples from Tesla, General Motors, The Kraft Heinz Company, and Kodak.

For over four decades, relationship management has been a concept studied in academia from various angles and widely applied in industry. Researchers from sociology, communication, psychology, and business studies have aimed to ascertain how corporations develop and maintain relationships with relevant stakeholder groups and what helps such relationships withstand the changes in the macrosystems in which companies operate. Undoubtedly, these relationships do not emerge in a vacuum, but rather in the context in which companies operate. Specifically, relationships are strategically developed and adapted to environmental variables, including the political economy that characterizes a macrosystem, its culture, the extant level of activism, and whether the media are free or controlled by the government (Verčič and Sriramesh 2019). For example, companies cannot successfully develop relationships without taking into consideration the activists' agenda and the degree to which it may impact operations should a company not meet such expectations. Furthermore, a government's control over the media system may hinder corporate efforts that aim to reach potential consumers through marketing and advertising campaigns, while the societal culture determines what communication practices are conducive to effective relationship development.

Above all, successful relationship management involves considering who a company's stakeholders are and taking into account the fact that groups and group dynamics change with the passage of time.

Successful relationship management involves considering who a company's stakeholders are and taking into account the fact that groups and group dynamics change with the passage of time.

According to stakeholder theory (Sagar Menghwar and Freeman 2023), companies should predominantly concentrate on their primary stakeholder groups on whom they depend for survival. Such groups include investors, employees, and consumers while secondary groups are represented by journalists, the government, trade unions, and activists. In recent years, as corporations in the United States have faced intense scrutiny and increased activism, researchers have argued that the communities that companies serve should also be regarded as a primary stakeholder group (McGahan 2023). Communication scholars simplified the identification of relevant stakeholders and argued that companies should develop and maintain mutually beneficial relationships with all the stakeholder groups that can impact a company and that, in turn, a company can impact through its operations and practices (Ledingham 2006; Place 2022; Zhan and Zhao 2023). This view implies that, in every business environment in which they operate, companies should regularly assess who their stakeholder groups are and the degree to which their expectations have changed. More precisely, while investors, employees, and consumers remain a corporation's fundamental stakeholders, certain secondary stakeholder groups may not play a central role at a given time or in a specific business environment. For example, activists may not constitute an important stakeholder group in countries with low levels of activism such as those of the Eastern world. In addition, in countries where the government owns the media, companies may not regard journalists as significant stakeholders and may focus on building relationships with the government since the latter exerts influence on media coverage.

Further, the expectations within any given stakeholder group change as membership evolves or the members' priorities shift. To remain viable, corporations should constantly assess stakeholder perceptions in an attempt to meet new expectations. In turn, meeting these expectations represents the sine qua non for successful relationships. Building and maintaining effective relationships in a corporate context is similar to the way we form relationships in our own lives. Namely, a successful relationship implies that our partner meets our expectations and fulfills our needs and that we reciprocate. In addition, both parties adapt to shifts in expectations as the needs of the other partner change. A business illustration of a shift in needs and expectations was the consumer focus on best mileage cars and electric cars that increased between 2020 and 2022. This shift was triggered by the state of the economy, inflation, as well as an increased consumer interest in environmental issues. Consequently, car manufacturers adapted to the new consumer preferences and were able to predict them by taking into account the variables of the economy (inflation) and activism (environmental concerns). Recently, car manufacturers have had to adapt again to the consumers' preferences for gas and hybrid vehicles after the sales of electric cars decreased.

The first step toward developing successful relationships represents the delivery of products and services that fulfill needs and meet expectations. Yet, in an extremely competitive market, the delivery of high-quality products may prove insufficient. To cut through the competition, corporations create an identity whose values are embedded in every internal function and structure and one that is promoted externally in all of the company's communications. The following sections of this chapter will provide details on what corporate identity represents and how companies create and promote it to manage stakeholder relationships.

Corporate Values and Corporate Identity

Founded in 2003 in San Carlos, California, Tesla's mission has been "to accelerate the world's transition to sustainable energy" by providing unparalleled products (Tesla 2023). To achieve this goal, Tesla established several corporate values, including respect for the environment, continued commitment to learning, respect and encouragement for people, and an emphasis on doing the best while realizing that no forecast is free of imperfections. The preceding values form Tesla's identity, an intangible asset (Gambetti, Melewar, and Martin 2017; Tourky, Kitchen, and Shaalan 2020). The identity makes the company recognizable and relatable to its stakeholder groups, therefore facilitating relationship development. At an internal level, these values enable employees to perform consistently and in line with the company's mission. For example, across Tesla's departments ranging from engineering to marketing, employees come to work knowing that they are expected to do their best and that the company understands when the outcome may not be what they initially expected. Put differently, in any department, employees know that they are allowed to fail and learn from errors as long as they always give their best. In turn, fostering this value facilitates innovation. Externally, the same value may lead consumers to understand that sustainable technology is still in its infancy and that, while the company has a dedicated team of employees, research toward perfection is ongoing. Finally, by establishing these values, Tesla appeals to job applicants who embrace the company's workplace environment and see themselves as part of its mission.

A company's values are avowed in its mission statement and lived out by its stakeholder groups through shopping experiences as well as exposure to marketing, public relations, advertising campaigns, and social media communication. At an internal level, employees are exposed to these values through trainings, orientation programs, and internal communications, among others. In addition, the employees experience them in their daily workplace interactions. Undoubtedly, every department will interpret a corporation's values according to its role and function, and every employee is likely to perceive them through their own lens. For example, a value like innovation will be perceived differently by employees working in research and development (R&D) than by those who work in HR. Similarly, external stakeholders may attribute different connotations to different values. Yet, by conducting regular employee and consumer surveys, companies can ensure that the interpretation of values does not significantly deviate from their identity. If significant deviations do occur, they signal the fact that the company needs to either make its identity clearer or shift the connotations of its values to meet stakeholder expectations. For example, one of Nike's values represents making it possible for everyone to achieve greatness. Hypothetically speaking, if Nike conducts a representative consumer survey and determines that the majority of the respondents regard the company's prices as too high, the company may reconsider its prices (adapt to the expectations of its consumers) or redefine the value by focusing on the achievement of greatness of a specific consumer such as semiprofessional athletes.

Companies generally prefer to define their values broadly enough to adapt them to different consumer expectations. Research refers to this process as strategic ambiguity (Eisenberg 1984). By defining their values ambiguously, corporations not only manage to adapt to changing stakeholder expectations but also accommodate various interpretations and enable a large number of stakeholders to perceive that there is a convergence between their values and those of the company. In the preceding Tesla example, the employees are aware that the company allows them to fail as long as they have given their best. Yet, giving one's best has different connotations for different employees. While some may consider that giving their best means making Tesla a quintessential part of their lives and ruminating on problem-solving even in their spare time, other employees may believe that they do their best if they are fully committed to their tasks from 9 to 5. In this case, the use of strategic ambiguity accommodates two different working styles, both of which benefit Tesla. Additionally, the use of strategic ambiguity creates bonds within the company as employees perceive that their definition of giving their best aligns with that of their colleagues and, therefore, they have much in common. In other words, strategic ambiguity unifies diverse perspectives (Eisenberg 1984) and bridges differences across the employee base.

However, companies should strike a balance between ambiguity and rigidity, the latter being particularly important with respect to the value of safety and in the context of businesses whose products and services can lead to significant harm. To illustrate value rigidity and its detrimental impact on business, consider Kodak, a brand that, sadly, Gen Z has hardly heard of. By defining itself as a company that makes memories possible through film, Kodak failed to innovate and embrace the digital camera. The company feared that by doing so it would go against its core value, which, in turn, would negatively impact profits. Finally, in 1996, the company launched its digital cameras. However, 15 years prior, Sony Corporation had already captured a market and branded themselves as the creators of the new photography. Consequently, in 2012, Kodak filed for bankruptcy (Abbas 2023; Gavetti, Henderson, and Giorgi 2004; Kmia 2023; Scheyder 2012).

If Kodak's case reveals value rigidity, Boeing's 2018 and 2019 crashes caused by its 737 MAX illustrate the result of top management framing the value of safety too ambiguously, as the company had focused on outcompeting Airbus. Media reports indicate that prior to these tragic crashes, the company had reduced the number of safety inspectors, rushed the production of the 737 MAX, and discouraged their employees from raising concerns by rejecting a proposal for safety upgrades (Gates 2019; Gates, Miletich, and Kamb 2019).

An additional example with respect to the negative impact of ambiguity is General Motors' ignition switch recall, which points to the misinterpretation of the imperative of "putting the company first." In 2014, it was revealed that a defective ignition switch had led to the death of 124 drivers (Isidore 2015). By March 2014, the company had recalled 2.6 million vehicles (Basu 2014) and ordered an external and unvarnished investigation into its operations. Among several noteworthy findings, the final report shed light on the ambiguity that emerged after the government had bailed out the company during the 2008 financial crisis. Management predominantly emphasized "putting the company first," and without a narrower definition, several employees across multiple departments attributed a different connotation to this value. Their interpretation of "putting the company first" led to the installation of a faulty ignition switch that was about to lead to tragedy. Moreover, in an attempt to put their company first, employees refrained from taking notes during safety-centered meetings and the very communication of "safety concerns" was supplanted by softer phrases, such as "issues of customer convenience" (Valukas 2014). In this case, several employees considered that putting the company first meant saving it from possible litigation and financial burden.

From Corporate Identity to Corporate Identification

In 1869, Henry Heinz, a 25-year-old son of Bavarian immigrants, opened a horseradish business in Sharpsburg, Pennsylvania. The financial crisis of 1873 shattered it, yet Heinz was determined to persevere. Three years later, with the financial help of his brother and cousin, he was able to reopen his business and launch a ketchup line. By the end of the 20th century, the business he founded, the H.J. Heinz Company, would reach global success, selling its products in more than 200 countries. Throughout his life, Henry Heinz acted as a champion for consumer protection and food quality and embraced what at that time represented a progressive leadership style. Namely, he provided his employees with benefits and amenities that were unheard of, including libraries, dining rooms, and roof gardens (Heinz History Center 2023). Today, his story of success informs the mission of the Kraft Heinz Company and is reflected in several of its values—daring to do better every day and doing the right thing by customers, partners, and communities. The values are ambiguous enough both to facilitate the identification of the stakeholders with the company and to enable the organization to adapt to a changing business environment. Above all, the values derive from Henry Heinz's story. Not only do they ensure a consistent corporate identity, but they also enable the company to easily promote them through storytelling.

It is worth noting that stakeholders are more likely to identify with a company that has a compelling story, with memorable plots and inspiring, yet relatable characters (Kent 2015). Stories facilitate the identification with a company because individuals are inherent storytellers (*homo narrans*) who, for thousands of years, have been making sense of the world around them through stories (Ahn 2021), have discussed past experiences through stories (Behrooz, Swanson, and Jhala 2015), and have related to others through stories.

Once exposed to Heinz's story, stakeholders find elements in the plot and traits in its main character that they can relate to. If stakeholders were exposed to a mere set of corporate values, they would be unlikely to remember them shortly afterwards. However, they will retain Heinz's story of success due to its memorability. The story depicts the journey of a man who transitions from a countryside boy into a business magnate. Its happy ending is made possible by the character's traits including determination, perseverance (Heinz reopened his company after the 1837 financial crisis destroyed it), and integrity (Heinz lobbied for consumer protection laws and was known as an innovator in food production quality). Each of us has a dream we want to pursue, whether it involves opening a business, learning to fly a plane, or studying medicine. Yet, the character's traits are applicable in every context and, therefore, Heinz is relatable and his journey memorable.

Thus far, we have discussed the importance of strategic ambiguity and storytelling in establishing and framing corporate values to facilitate corporate identification. Corporate identification constitutes the first step toward building relationships as stakeholders perceive that, to some extent, their own values converge with those of a company. More specifically, a company and its stakeholders have something in common that goes beyond products and services. Once identification occurs, stakeholders and companies find themselves in what can be considered a parasocial relationship, a concept discussed next.

Parasocial relationships are one-way relationships that stakeholders develop with companies. A similar phenomenon is found in the case of celebrities and sports teams. Stakeholders perceive that, given the convergence between their personal values and those espoused by a company, they know and understand the organization. In turn, the company understands them too, as evident in the products and services that it delivers that meet stakeholder needs, in its social media communication that is approachable and humorous, and in the advertising campaigns that mirror the consumers' culture and preferences. Such relationships are one way because, while an Apple enthusiast may identify with the company, it is impossible for a corporate giant like Apple to know every specific consumer. Companies know and understand their consumers through large datasets that are analyzed to determine preferences and behavior (Lee and Kwangho 2023; Liao, Bin Lin, Haiyan, and Xi 2021; Yuan and Chen 2020).

For the purpose of brevity, this book will refer to parasocial relationships as stakeholder relationships. The relationships between stakeholders and companies form as a result of commonalities (a convergence of values) and problem-solving (a consumer has a need that a company satisfies through the delivery of products/services; a job applicant needs a certain position in the field that the company offers). Once established, relationships are fostered through action and communication, both of which are meant to maintain trust and ensure the longevity of the relationships. Action means that companies need to deliver what they have avowed in their mission statement and live by the values and the identity that they have created. Stakeholders view a company that doesn't act consistently as unpredictable and, therefore, unworthy of trust. Moreover, the company's communication practices, whether on social media or offline (in stores and face-to-face customer service interactions) have to involve openness and dialogue, therefore mimicking the interactions that generally comprise successful relationships in everyday life. In the next chapters, we will explore how dialogue and openness instill trust and what the main ingredients of successful communication represent in the case of external and internal stakeholder groups and local and international business environments.

CHAPTER 2

Employee Relationships and Corporate Identification

This chapter is dedicated to internal relationship management and employee identification with a company. The first part discusses the role of corporate values in recruiting job applicants and in triggering their identification with their employer. The chapter then tackles the role of corporate values and corporate identification in fostering a positive internal culture. Finally, the last section will expose the reader to how internal social media platforms can be used to strengthen relationships across the employee base via corporate values. As a practical application, the chapter discusses the sexual harassment scandal at Microsoft.

New Employees and Corporate Identification

It has become common practice for corporations to look for employees who can "fit in" or adapt to a specific workplace environment. Simply put, every company aims to recruit employees who would work toward fulfilling the mission of the company while adapting to the office atmosphere. This implies that applicants' qualifications are insufficient unless the individuals display that, to some degree, and their personal values align with the company's. It is the role of HR officers to ask interview questions that would shed light on whether the applicant's understanding of a corporate value such as "passion" aligns with what the company is expecting. Undoubtedly, an astute applicant would meticulously prepare for the interview and possibly determine beforehand how the corporation's values would apply to their position and qualifications. Yet, if the applicant doesn't display sincerity during the interview and obtains the position, it is probable that the relationship with the company will be short-lived. This happens because the internal culture or the atmosphere in the workplace is built around corporate values the new employee may find it hard to adapt to.

Hypothetically speaking, Jane Doe, a software engineer, is hired by Microsoft. At the job interview, Jane proves to be a remarkable engineer. She displays several of Microsoft's values: she loves to innovate, appreciates the variety of perspectives that stem from working in a diverse environment, and values philanthropy. During the orientation day, Jane and several other new employees from various departments are introduced to the company's values, its history, and its mission. Jane is delighted to learn that today's Big Tech superstar started in an Albuquerque garage back in 1975 as friends Bill Gates and Allen Paul decided to create revolutionary software (McFadden 2020). Bill Gates's focus on innovation, his journey toward global success, and his passion for philanthropy inform the present corporate values and ensure consistency. Jane's orientation reinforces the fact that she made a good decision when she accepted Microsoft's job offer.

Jane's identification with the company starts on her orientation day. So does her parasocial relationship with Microsoft and with the founder of the company. She feels that she has a good insight into both, she understands them, and, in turn, they understand their employees. Next, Jane is likely to draw on the company's powerful brand for social recognition (Hastwell 2022). Specifically, she may talk to her friends and family about Microsoft often because she takes pride in working for the powerful tech giant, worldwide known not only for the IT revolution it engendered but also for being highly selective in its recruitment. Microsoft's identity becomes part of Jane's identity as she draws on the former to gain recognition outside the workplace.

During her orientation day, Jane meets John Doe, a new employee in the public relations department. She asks him about his work and he describes his focus on graphic design for communication campaigns. John innovates too, yet differently from Jane. Their conversation, which starts around their work, moves on to topics such as the universities they attended, prior employers, and hobbies. This scenario illustrates how two new employees first bonded around Microsoft and its value of innovation. Subconsciously, they bond over a corporate value and the ongoing conversation reveals they have more and more in common. If they continue to interact, it is likely that the information exchanges will strengthen their bond as each party reveals more about themselves. In communication theory, this process is referred to as social penetration (Low et al. 2022). Two interlocutors are likely to reveal more about themselves, including personal information as the interaction progresses. The more they reveal about themselves the stronger the bond between them and the less likely they are to end these interactions. It is worth mentioning that interactions may cease at any given time should one party reveal significantly less about themselves than the other (Carpenter and Greene 2015; Mangus et al. 2020).

The collegial relationship between Jane and John is representative of what takes place in the corporate world as employees identify with the company through its values and their own. Next, they identify with other colleagues since the employee base is rooted in these values. Consequently, the employees have a lot in common: they display the unified diversity (Eisenberg 1984) discussed in Chapter 1. A company and its employees find themselves in a parasocial relationship given that, as an entity, a corporation can never know and understand each and every employee. Yet, an employee may perceive that it does, and a company fosters this perception through recognition events, holiday parties, benefits, and amenities. By contrast, relationships as we know them in everyday life emerge among employees and are fostered through a positive internal culture that is discussed next.

The Internal Culture

For the purpose of consistency and to ensure that employees work toward fulfilling the company's mission, management aims to create an internal culture that revolves around the corporation's values. Known as the atmosphere at the workplace, the internal culture is regularly referenced in the corporate world as "how we do things around here." It comprises rites, rituals, stories, beliefs, and behavioral expectations, to name a few. One ritual that may characterize an internal culture could be a regular and informal get-together that the employees have every Friday upon finishing work. Additionally, stories abound in corporations, particularly in departments that regularly interact with customers, and humorous instances are passed from veteran employees to new hires. Communication styles, dress codes, high versus low power distance relationships between management and employees, and office arrangements represent additional elements that form an internal culture. It could be argued that the internal culture comprises two layers: a visible layer and an invisible one (Luu, Nguyen, and Wilson 2023; Schein 2009). The visible layer constitutes everything that one can observe when walking into the headquarters of a corporation for the first time. Office layouts and decorations, posters, and furniture arrangements, if observed closely, provide an insight into the workplace atmosphere. Specifically, a manager's office with a desk placed to block the space between themselves and the employees during meetings connotes high power distance and indicates a top-down approach to leadership. Further, international customer service call centers that serve American corporations decorate their spaces with artifacts such as American flags and sports memorabilia in an attempt to mimic aspects of the American culture that would enable foreign employees to appropriately communicate with U.S.-based consumers. The visible layer of the internal culture represents an attempt to help customer service representatives understand the American mindset and adopt an American approach to problem-solving. Finally, if you walk into an office and you notice no personal items such as family pictures or similar personal items, it may be an indication that the employee does not feel comfortable at the workplace and, therefore, draw a distinct line between the personal and the professional. This, in turn, might be an indication of a possible future departure from the company.

By contrast, the invisible layer of the internal culture remains something that a new employee discovers in time. It subsumes cultural aspects that range from behavioral expectations to intrinsic vernacular. Both the invisible and the visible layers are initially triggered by management through the promotion of corporate values. Yet, while new employees are initially exposed to a corporation's values during orientation, once they commence working, the employees become an intrinsic part of the internal culture which they may find not perfectly aligned with management's definition of the values. This happens because the interactions that Jane and John have today will differ from those that will take place in a few months as their experiences have changed. Specifically, how they approach innovation in their work may change and so may the way they communicate about it. Consequently, the internal culture is in continued transformation because the employees themselves undergo change. For this reason, management cannot exert the utmost influence over the internal culture.

Management triggers a certain culture by defining the corporate values of the culture. Yet, employees socially construct these values, shape them, and shift their connotations through daily interactions. Corporations can regularly conduct internal surveys that assess how employees perceive the company's values. If the results show significant deviations from the corporate identity, companies have to conduct formal and informal trainings, meetings, and organized events that will ensure that the employees perceive the company as more in line with its mission.

The importance of a positive internal culture cannot be overstated. It motivates employees, engenders loyalty, and bolsters their identification with the company. Moreover, it increases collaboration which, in turn, leads to enhanced creativity and innovation (Mahdy, Alqahtani, and Binzafrah 2023; Sabuhari et al. 2020). Finally, a positive internal culture determines a constant flow of valuable information that can entail supportive messages and promotion tips, all of which were found in past research studies to be conducive to the retention of diverse employees who oftentimes feel that they lack connections in the workplace (Maiorescu-Murphy 2019).

Companies can foster a positive internal culture through employee recognition events, internal newsletters, internal websites dedicated to employee affairs, and event planning, among others. In addition to regular compensations and benefits, these efforts make employees feel valued and appreciated. Since the advent of Web 2.0, corporations have transitioned some of their efforts online, as discussed next.

Internal Relationships and Social Media

Today companies make extensive use of social media platforms and use software designed specifically for internal purposes. Slack is a well-known example, yet corporations oftentimes opt for customized platforms that are adapted to their specific needs. These social media tools are not made public but are available only to their employees.

The purpose of these platforms is to foster parasocial relationships between the employees and the company and to maintain a positive internal culture by cultivating workplace relationships online. Offline companies try to foster internal cultures reminiscent of the family spirit, while social media platforms enable them to create or strengthen the already-established bonds among their employees. These bonds can lead to the formation of an online community of collaboration, support, and information-sharing. Corporations attempt to create what research refers to as online communities. The results of past studies on the business use of online communities (Kim et al. 2023; Kwon and Ha 2023) suggest several implications for the internal use of social media platforms.

Let's leave aside the instances in which companies require their employees to join internal social media platforms and let's focus on situations in which employees join these communication channels willingly, namely as a result of their identification with the company. The concept is called identity-based attachment (Lee and Hsieh 2022). It implies that corporate identification will lead the employees to engage in regular and significant online communication with their employer. An important advantage of internal social media platforms is their potential to connect employees from across multiple countries and regions, which is particularly important for a conglomerate giantlike General Motors, for example. The company has over 167,000 employees across the globe, most of whom would never have the opportunity to connect outside an online platform. With time and regular interactions, employees who communicate online are likely to form a bond that continues to strengthen with the regular use of social media communication. Hence, social media facilitates the transition from identity-based attachment (identification with the company) to bond-based attachment (relationships among the employees).

The transition from identity-based attachment to bond-based attachment mirrors the exact process that occurs in the workplace as Jane and John get to know their colleagues, find commonalities, and create relationships through constant interactions. Such relationships may develop quicker and may evolve into deeper connections than offline. This happens because the internet erases social markers such as ethnicity, gender, and race (Maiorescu-Murphy 2019; Matei and Bruno 2015) and can lead to the establishment of stronger bonds among employees who unite online around a common interest: the corporation. It is important to mention that bonds created online have the potential to translate into workplace interactions, namely, employees who develop a relationship on an internal social media platform and who have the opportunity to meet in person will do so. This, in turn, might strengthen their relationship.

Additionally, self-disclosure takes place more rapidly in online settings than in face-to-face interactions, a possible effect of the erasure of social markers, a focus on commonalities (the company), and the fact that online users do not perceive the implications of their communication with the gravity they would offline (Maiorescu-Murphy 2019). Therefore, it is likely that, from the perspective of the social penetration theory, social media platforms hasten the development of employee relationships. In turn, the relationships developed online contribute to a positive internal culture. For example, research studies showed that as the number of bonds in an online community continues to increase, its members display social capital (Fenton, Gillooly, and Vasilica 2023), namely, employees have a reservoir of collective resources and valuable information they can share and draw on collectively to help one another in the workplace.

An illustrative example of collective help is what transpired in Microsoft's sexual harassment scandal that emerged in 2019 on an internal server. A female employee's post concerning her inability to be promoted prompted a significant discussion thread that brought to light instances of sexual harassment along with solutions as to how the employees should collectively broach the topic with the CEO and what steps they should take to ensure their concern could reach the upper echelons (Gershgorn 2019). The social capital they drew on led to significant steps by Microsoft to ensure a workplace environment free of sexual harassment and high on accountability. This example additionally illustrates the potential of internal social media platforms to reveal employee issues if companies regularly scan their input. A regular assessment of employee online communication can help companies address issues before these turn into crises.

The development of online communities requires a significant amount of time and resources. Many corporations believe that they are successful at this attempt, yet such conclusions would require an assessment of the degree to which employees who regularly interact online (1) are familiar with one another and (2) are familiar with past topics discussed online (Hennig-Thurau et al. 2004; Moon, Seung-Wook, and Iacobucci 2023). For example, if John Doe is a regular contributor, in how many of the posts he made during the last month did he refer other users to past content posted online? Finally, in how many of his posts did John seem to remember other users' hobbies, work projects, and so on?

The strategy behind building an online community is not intricate. To transform an internal social media platform into a community, a group of communication professionals should start interacting with one another regularly. The communication process should be transparent and should entail informing the employees (online users) of the aim and benefits of creating an online community. Genuine communication engenders increased contributions, and the constant posts and responses of the communication team will in time lead to increased interactions. The posts should be informative, yet casual to align with the expectations that online users have in terms of social media communication. To effectively reach employees, the posts should reflect the internal culture. Therefore, it is essential for communication professionals to closely observe the internal culture, the employee's rites, rituals, and their vernacular in order to effectively emulate them in online posts. In addition, some of the posts should reflect the company's values to appeal to the employees' identity-based attachment.

The online communication process through which relationships with employees are developed online involves a blend of informative (one-way) posts and questions (two-way communication). Analogous to the establishment of relationships with employees offline, each party incorporates the feedback it receives to accommodate the needs of the other. In other words, corporations should entertain a feedback loop that would not only make their employees feel valuable and useful, but it would also enable companies to improve and adapt to changes in employee expectations.

To conclude, this chapter has taken an internal approach to building and maintaining offline and online relationships. Corporations aim to build a positive internal culture that can be further bolstered via online communities. In turn, a positive internal culture and a solid online community engender major advantages for both companies and their employees. While corporations gain employee motivation, commitment, increased productivity, and loyalty, employees benefit from social rewards, including validation, respect, and opportunity. Above all, the relationships that the employees build across the online base enable them to gain access to valuable information and resources.

CHAPTER 3

Leadership and Employee Relationships

Undoubtedly, leaders exert tremendous influence over the internal culture, the development of employee relationships, and the extent to which employees identify with their company. The present chapter explores the role of specific leadership and communication styles in accomplishing positive outcomes. Furthermore, the chapter applies several theoretical concepts to practice by providing examples from Microsoft and General Motors. It analyzes the leadership styles of the companies' CEOs, Satya Nadella and Mary Barra.

Leadership Styles and Corporate Identity

In 2014, Satya Nadella became Microsoft's third CEO. In addition to his extensive experience and expertise, which ranges from electrical and computer engineering to business, Nadella brought along a genuine commitment to creating a workplace that would be accessible for people with disabilities and to releasing products that fulfill the same mission (Disability: IN 2023). In 2017, he published the book entitled *Hit Refresh: The Quest to Rediscover Microsoft's Soul and Imagine a Better Future for Everyone*. In the book, he discussed his leadership style and his focus on changing Microsoft's internal culture. Further, he exposed the reader to the challenges of a dedicated father and to his commitment to finding every possible solution to help his son, Zain, and others whose lives are impacted by cerebral palsy:

> Becoming a father of a son with special needs was the turning point in my life that has shaped who I am today. It has helped me better understand the journey of people with disabilities. It has shaped my personal passion for and philosophy of

connecting new ideas to empathy for others. And it is why I am deeply committed to pushing the bounds ... with my colleagues at Microsoft. (Nadella 2017)

As Satya Nadella took the helm of Microsoft, his dedication to assisting people with special needs intertwined with Microsoft's values of corporate social responsibility (CSR), diversity and inclusion, and innovation. To date, Microsoft has offered various inclusive products and services, including immersive readers for students with dyslexia and learning differences, speech-to-text tools for individuals with limited mobility, and a range of products to assist people with vision, hearing, and mobility challenges (Microsoft 2023).

Similar to the recruitment of the employee base, the selection of a CEO is significantly influenced by their personal values and the degree to which they intertwine with those of a company. Yet, in Satya Nadella's case, these values have deeper connotations and derive from a personal journey that has informed his priorities and influenced his leadership style. His dedication to innovating for a higher cause than mere business growth has led to the development of strong parasocial relationships. Such parasocial relationships develop twofold: between the CEO and the employee base and between the employee and the company. Specifically, Microsoft employees who may never have the opportunity to meet Nadella in person understand his journey and may feel that, given the empathy that characterizes his leadership style, he can, in turn, understand them. This is illustrated by employees' reactions to the sexual harassment scandal that Microsoft faced in 2019, as referred to in Chapter 2. As employees communicated their frustration with the company on an internal server and X (formerly Twitter), they planned to bring the situation to the attention of the CEO. They were certain that the complaints that they had previously filed with HR never reached the highest levels. The employees' communication denoted trust in their leader and their certainty that, if Nadella had been previously made aware of the sexual harassment in their workplace, he would have uprooted it. Finally, these online interactions showed that the employees trusted that given his values, the CEO would show impartiality in the internal investigation.

The preceding communication examples shed light on a solid parasocial relationship with the CEO which, in turn, triggers the employees' identification with the company. Whether the employees know Nadella through personal encounters or merely through digital communications, for many of them, he represents Microsoft. Further, research shows that employees are more likely to embrace the causes that their leaders espouse when they perceive that these causes revolve around morality (Lee and Tao 2021) rather than business interests. Arguably, Satya Nadella's commitment to advancing technology for special needs is deeply rooted in morality. In recent years, there has been much criticism of corporations, and companies have been placed under the magnifying glass for their operations and practices. Yet, no critic, however harsh, could deny the recent societal contributions made by Microsoft, not only in assisting with neurodiversity but also in raising awareness and removing stigmas.

As pointed out, Microsoft's CEO attributes his empathetic leadership style to his personal journey. His approach connotes a transformational leadership style, known to motivate employees to embrace their leaders' values and causes (Lee and Tao 2021). The transformational leadership style is exhibited (Bakker et al. 2023; Bass and Riggio 2010) by executives who lead their employees toward positive group thinking as opposed to self-centeredness and inspire them to achieve success through a solid vision, well-defined objectives, and intellectual stimulation. By serving as role models, transformational leaders effectively persuade employees that their vision for the corporation will lead to achievement for the organization and individuals. The leaders' enthusiasm is contagious and permeates the internal culture to the point where employees are "transformed" and become an integral part of a collective working toward fulfilling the leader's vision. Above all, transformational leadership involves the constant intellectual challenging of the employees who are asked to provide critique and feedback on decision making without fear of repercussions (Bakker et al. 2023).

According to media coverage of Microsoft's 2019 scandal, the company's CEO held multiple employee forums to discuss solutions that would lead to a change in the internal culture and the eradication of sexual harassment in the workplace. Undoubtedly, this approach to problem-solving is indicative of the transformational leadership style and is an effective way to find the best solutions for change. Namely, the employees who were impacted by sexual harassment are the ones who can find the best solutions for its eradication. Their participation in the decision-making process and their empowerment thereof may play a decisive role in whether they decide to leave the company or continue their tenure in the hopes that the corporation has learned from its transgressions. Generally, when employees take an active part in corporate decision-making processes, they identify with their company more strongly.

By contrast, the transactional leadership style assumes that a manager or executive focuses on the individual achievement of the employees and rewards or deprives them of social, psychological, or financial benefits based on their performance (Mekonnen and Bayissa 2023). Hence, employee-management relationships are established through a top-down process and are likely to be positive for the employees who consistently perform at a high level. The least encountered leadership style represents servant leadership, which is generally present in the case of managers and executives who founded a company or whose families have been connected to a corporation through generational employment. Servant leadership is exclusively employee-centered as opposed to the transformational leadership style that balances employee welfare with corporate interests (Meuser and Smallfield 2023). In practice, an executive may display a dominant leadership style, whether transformational, transactional, or servant. Yet, the application of a leadership style is situational. A manager who has a prevalent transformational leadership style is likely to enact a transactional style as the company goes through a financial crisis and in interactions with employees who are underperforming. Overall, a multitude of research studies showed that transformational leadership successfully fosters relationships between employees and leaders. In turn, the bonds established with the help of transformational leadership trigger a higher identification with the company and have a positive impact on employee morale, loyalty, well-being, and performance.

Leadership and Internal Cultures

In leadership literature, there is an old dictum that says "leadership and internal culture are two sides of the same coin" (Schein 2009, 3). Specifically, by fostering quality relationships with employees, leaders exert influence on a positive internal culture. (Undoubtedly, the opposite holds true as well.) In turn, a positive internal culture determines higher identification with a company and its leaders, as employees who feel valued and appreciated are more likely to identify with a corporation's mission and work toward fulfilling it. High employee identification with a company's leaders ensures that managers have the support they need across the employee base, a fact that proves crucial in times of financial turmoil or in crises such as product recalls and accidents.

During the 2014 ignition switch recall, GM's CEO Mary Barra created the "Speak Up for Safety" program to motivate and reward employees for promptly alerting management to safety concerns.

Mary Barra explained her decision as follows:

GM must embrace a culture where safety and quality come first ... GM employees should raise safety concerns quickly and forcefully, and be recognized for doing so. ... We will recognize employees who discover and report safety issues to fix problems that could have been found earlier and identify ways to make vehicles safer. (General Motors Newsroom 2014)

To speed up the cultural change at GM and increase participation in the "Speak Up for Safety" program, the CEO asked the employees to directly email her with safety concerns. As the ignition switch crisis was unfolding, she took the time to personally respond to every email. By doing so, Mary Barra empowered employees to become an integral part of the crisis management process. In other words, everyone at

GM brought their contribution to addressing the crisis and ensuring that it represented a one-time negative event whose lessons constituted an opportunity for the company's renewal. The "Speak Up for Safety" program was initiated while an external investigation ordered by GM into its ignition switch was still unfolding. Hence, the CEO addressed the crisis promptly, even before the investigation had been completed. She argued that consumers would judge the company not by the crisis itself but by how swiftly GM addressed it. Mary Barra's vision for GM's crisis management and the company's renewal has led to its current market success. Specifically, since General Motors addressed its ignition switch, it has become the leading automaker in the United States, surpassing Wall Street expectations (Toeppe 2023). Brian Kuney, vice president of Manufacturing Extension Partnership, attributed GM's success to "collaborative leadership" and "a collaborative culture" (Toeppe 2023).

Barra, who had been appointed CEO a few months before the ignition switch crisis emerged, demonstrated a transformational leadership style that involved a vision for General Motors: maintaining consumer trust. To achieve this, she made consumer safety a priority. However, this required a change in the internal culture and, generally, internal cultures are hard to change. This happens because, after years at the workplace, the employees' beliefs and patterns of behavior become deeply ingrained. This fact gives rise to the frequently heard phrase, "But we've always done it this way." Swift changes in internal cultures can only occur when leaders specifically ask the employees to alter behaviors and rituals and when leaders themselves act as role models. As Barra aimed to build safety into GM's internal culture, she predominantly used a transformational leadership style: she delivered a vision and acted as a role model. The fact that she personally responded to employee concerns regarding safety denotes a servant leadership style. Finally, two engineers who were found responsible for the negligence that led to the ignition switch recall were placed on leave, a decision that denotes a transactional leadership style. Consequently, she predominantly displayed a transformational leadership style and embraced transactional and servant approaches as required by the situation.

Above all, GM's CEO successfully managed to create internal change as employees quickly embraced her vision, partly because of her tremendous expertise and work experience as well as the relationships that she had previously developed across the company. Before she became CEO, Barra had worked in various departments at GM that ranged from engineering, product development, communications, and human resources (McGregor 2014). Not only did she gain invaluable experience in her various assignments, but she also garnered the support and appreciation of her co-workers.

Research from the realm of business studies enables us to take a closer look at what employee-leadership relationships entail and what makes them effective. For example, the leader-member exchange (LMX) theory considers that high versus low-quality exchanges between leaders and employees trigger high versus low performance. The exchanges that take between the two parties may be social (moral support, encouragement, respect, perceived job security, etc.) and economic (bonuses, promotion, increased benefits, etc.). In recent research that evaluated face-to-face interactions between leaders and employees, social exchanges played a role in the employees' well-being while the frequency of these interactions exerted less influence (Martin et al. 2023). These findings imply that in order to foster high-quality relationships, managers do not necessarily have to dedicate a significant amount of time to regularly interact with their employees. However, when they do so, they have to provide supportive communication and engage in active listening, both of which ultimately motivate employees and enable them to view themselves as an integral part of their company's life.

Leader-member exchanges are not static but fluctuate (Martin 2023), given the fact that the dynamics of the relationships may change. For example, an employee may enjoy a high-quality relationship with a leader that may devolve into a low-quality one as both parties undergo change. For example, an employee may become less committed to work, in which case the leader is likely to reduce the number of social and economic exchanges. It is worth mentioning that given the power distance extant between leaders and employees, it is the leaders that generally initiate exchanges rather than the employees.

Additionally, employees, who are in a high-quality relationship with a leader and witness a low-quality interaction between one of their colleagues and the same leader, are likely to not hold the leader in the same high regard as they did before (Cropanzano, Dasborough, and Weiss 2017). This reaction is caused by the perceived double standards that are likely to make the employee question whether the leader's attitude is free from pretense. While it is common for leaders to foster high-quality and low-quality exchanges based on the employees' high versus low performance, they should avoid inconsistency when interacting with multiple employees in one setting.

Finally, research on LMX determined that high-quality exchanges lead employees to identify with a corporation and to support its mission and causes (Loi, Chan, and Lam 2014). To refer back to the ignition switch recall, the previously fostered high-quality exchanges between CEO Barra and GM's employees facilitated the latter's identification with GM, particularly as she envisioned a renewed company after the crisis. Hence, it was the employees' trust in her and their previously developed relationships that triggered corporate identification at a time when the company was facing a congressional hearing and significant negative media coverage, all of which could have led to low employee morale and detachment from corporate values.

In sum, corporate culture, corporate identification, and relationship management intertwine in organizational life. Leaders can foster corporate identification and exert influence on the internal culture (changing or shaping it) by fostering relationships that revolve around high-quality exchanges with their employees. Research on the use of internal social media platforms to foster leader-member exchanges is still in its infancy. Yet, its results indicate that when leaders have already developed relationships with their employees via face-to-face interactions, they can use internal social media platforms to bolster these relationships. The use of social media platforms for this purpose leads to higher employee well-being and higher motivation (Goh and Wasko 2012; Varma et al. 2022). However, much remains to be learned about whether leader-employee social media interactions can trigger similar positive effects when the two parties have not yet interacted face-to-face.

CHAPTER 4

Crisis Management and Employee Relationships

The current chapter explores crisis management and its impact on employee relationships and identification with a company. Corporations enact multiple strategies whose aim is to diminish the negative impact of a crisis. These communication strategies are explained by looking at negative events faced by Johnson & Johnson (J&J), Disney, and France Telecom (FT). While the first part of the chapter discusses the impact of crises on employee identification, the following sections deal with instances in which the employees' strong identification with their company led to crises.

Crisis Management and Employee Identification

Let's take a look at J&J's ongoing talc powder crisis. Since 2009, when the company faced its first lawsuit for the alleged sales of talc powder that caused ovarian cancer, J&J has seen several legal defeats. For example, in 2016, the company was ordered to pay $72 million, and two years later a jury reached a $4.69 billion verdict for victim compensation (Buntz 2023). Recently, the number of complaints has reached 51,000 (Feeley 2023). In September 2023, as the lawsuits against J&J had increased by 28 percent, the Court rejected the company's attempt to settle the case for $9 billion through the bankruptcy of its LTL management unit that J&J had previously created for victim compensation (Feeley 2023).

A closer look at J&J's crisis management as presented in the media shows that since the 1970s, the company had been under scrutiny for the potential presence of asbestos in its talcum powder (Llamas 2023). In September 2019, out of an abundance of caution, J&J recalled a batch of over 30,000 bottles after the FDA had found small traces of asbestos in one bottle. In 2023, the company decided to cease the commercialization of its talc powder worldwide (Llamas 2023). J&J argued that its decision represented a discontinuation of the product rather than a recall, triggered by waning sales as opposed to safety concerns. Moreover, corporate representatives asserted that the decrease in sales constituted a consequence of misinformation and litigation advertising (Llamas 2023).

Based on the information available in the media and the statements that J&J made publicly, the company aimed to maintain consumer trust by taking a proactive step rather than issuing a recall. Moreover, throughout the crisis, J&J made regular statements to update the public and refute what it regarded as disparaging information, particularly since it found contradictions between its safety results and the media coverage. The company took preemptive action and engaged in constant communication, two strategies conducive to maintaining consumer trust. Based on the information presently available, there has been no investigation or trial that linked J&J to embedding asbestos in its talc powder. Neither has there been evidence with regard to the company's attempts to conceal safety concerns from the public. Yet, J&J's crisis could not have been averted. The fact that asbestos was found in solely one bottle might constitute an accident. However, an avalanche of lawsuits and negative media coverage led to the demise of the product.

According to crisis management research, the type of crisis a company faces (whether a crisis the company could have prevented or an accident) generally determines the degree of responsibility that stakeholders attribute to the corporation (Coombs 2020, 2022). However, in the case of J&J, the responsibility attribution that the public assigned to the company was enhanced by emotions, as talc powder had been a landmark product for babies since the 50s. Stakeholders process crisis information cognitively and emotionally (Coombs and Tachkova 2023). When emotions take precedence over cognitions, consumers are more inclined to seek revenge on a corporation by boycotting its products and spreading negative word-of-mouth as they perceive that the corporation committed a breach of trust or morality (Coombs and Tachkova 2018).

Even if a company may not be responsible for a crisis, the negative media coverage and the negative word-of-mouth spread particularly on social media can take a toll on its employees. As employees are exposed to these communications online and in their daily lives, they may cease to draw on the company's brand to gain outside recognition. Specifically, they no longer publicly take pride in representing the company irrespective of the degree to which they still identify with it. As discussed in Chapter 1, powerful brands lead employees to draw on the former's visibility and recognition to gain social recognition outside the workplace. However, while generally, employees who display high corporate identification take pride in their workplace and positively communicate about their company in social circles (Hastwell 2022), they may cease to do so when their employer faces an influx of negative media coverage.

No information is available about the way J&J addressed the crisis internally. As a rule of thumb, companies should inform their employees about a crisis before the media first covers it. When the employees learn about a crisis from a third party, the relationship they have developed with the company is jeopardized and their identification with their employer may decrease. They feel betrayed as they perceive that their opinions and expertise in helping the company address a crisis are not valued. Moreover, learning about a crisis from the press erodes trust as employees wonder about additional covert issues that the media may reveal about their employer in the near future. This, in turn, triggers speculation in the workplace that impacts daily interactions as employees try to make sense of the crisis and spread rumors. When a company finally acknowledges the crisis internally, it has already lost control over it. By covering the crisis first, the media defined it for the employees. In this case, it is extremely hard for corporations to regain control over the narrative and persuasively redefine the crisis. Because no information is available about the way J&J handled the talc powder crisis internally, let's assume two scenarios: one in which the company informs its employees about the crisis before the publication of the first news article and the second, a scenario in which employees learn about the crisis from the media.

In the first scenario, J&J's employees would feel valued and respected because the company reached out to them first. In addition, the employees' identification with the company remains strong particularly as, by informing the employee base first, the company controls the narrative and, therefore, maintains their trust. As noted previously, the media's coverage of the crisis deviated from J&J's perspective, making it even more imperative to reach out to the employees first. When communicating about the crisis to their employees, companies should also relay the specifics of the media coverage they anticipate receiving. Namely, communication professionals should view the crisis from the perspective of multiple stakeholder groups, including journalists, consumers, and activists, and ascertain what rumors and speculation may emerge that could set the media's agenda. Relaying this information to the employees prepares them to receive news that is contrary to their beliefs and the reality of the present crisis.

Communication research refers to this proactive process as "inoculation" and what better way to explain it than in the context of a pharmaceutical company like J&J? Similar to the way one is immunized against a virus or disease, companies present their employees in times of crisis with information the organization anticipates may come from third parties. This information is assumed to run contrary to the actual situation that the company is experiencing (Compton, Wigley, and Samoilenko 2021). By doing so, companies prepare their employees to refute contradictory information. Above all, by reaching out to their employees, companies can make them an integral part of the crisis management process. Employee input and recommendations can prove invaluable in addressing crises. In turn, by contributing to their company's decision-making, employees feel empowered and valuable, all of which strengthen their corporate identification.

Studies show that the foremost expectation that employees have from their company represents opportunities to actively contribute to their employer through knowledge, skills, expertise, and so on, and to have such contributions recognized (Windscheid et al. 2017). Therefore, crises represent opportunities to make employees a part of the decision-making process. Above all, throughout this process, employees and management collectively decide on the corrective action that the company should take to address the crisis, and given that such action needs to align with a company's values, crises represent opportunities to bolster the identification of the employees with the company and strengthen relationships across the employee base. For employee engagement during crises, companies can use internal social media platforms, polls, and open-question surveys.

By contrast, since trust and open communication represent the main ingredients of successful relationship management, it is not surprising that learning about your company's crisis through the media is likely to lead to low employee morale, decreased identification with the company, and reduced workplace productivity. Hence, if we consider the second hypothetical scenario and assume that J&J's employees learned about the talc powder crisis from the media, we can infer that an internal survey would reveal lower levels of trust in the company's leadership and values. This scenario would run contrary to the very values that J&J had espoused, including responsibility to doctors, nurses, mothers, fathers, and everyone who uses the company's products. Such findings would constitute the consequence of a lack of transparency and lead the employees to perceive that their company finds their contributions irrelevant. When coupled with personal experiences in the workplace that are less than positive, perceptions of irrelevance can lead to dissatisfaction and turnover.

Employee Identification and Crises

While J&J's crisis and the two hypothetical scenarios we considered may indirectly impact employee identification with the company, there are multiple examples of crises in other organizations that were caused by corporate identification. Specifically, after years in which the upper echelons facilitated the interpretation of corporate values in ways that benefitted the company, management switched gears as the company underwent financially turbulent times. This decision led to high turnover as the employees no longer recognized their workplace and, at times, had tragic consequences as discussed next.

In 2019, three of France Telecom's (FT) former top executives, including the company's ex-CEO, his second in command, and the former director of HR were sentenced to four months in prison for institutional moral harassment, which led to the suicide of 35 FT employees (Nossiter 2019). The employees died by suicide or attempted suicide in mid-2000s. The criminal court in Paris found the three executives responsible for the creation of a toxic atmosphere in the workplace as they attempted to fire nearly 22,000 employees in response to the company's $50 billion debt (Nossiter 2019). The court found that creating a toxic corporate culture represented an illegitimate means by which the executives attempted to let go of over 18 percent of their employee base (Nossiter 2019). During the trial, FT employees provided graphic information about the despair of their colleagues who attempted suicide or died by it, either at or outside the workplace, resorting to desperate measures out of fear and anxiety they experienced, particularly after having been assigned to roles they were not suited for (Nossiter 2019). For example, in a botched attempt at restructuring, the company forced technicians into sales positions (Nossiter 2019), reduced opportunities for promotion, and placed increased pressure on the employee base as the market had already been saturated by telecom services. In the former CEO's words that were cited in Court, these measures were meant to get the employees out "by the window or the door" (Nossiter 2019). Witnesses described the ordeal experienced by colleagues who threw themselves out of the windows or under trains and bridges, set themselves on fire (Nossiter 2019), and stabbed themselves during a management meeting (Chrisafis 2009).

Prior to experiencing financial turmoil that required restructuring, FT instilled in its employees the importance of putting the customer first and ensuring their satisfaction, even at the expense of telecom subscriptions. As the European market became saturated with mobile phones and services, the company shifted gears and placed pressure on its employees to increase sales. This led to a clash between the identity of the company as avowed in its mission statement and previously experienced by the employees and the aggression with which FT later pursued sales at all costs. The positive atmosphere in the workplace that had been fostered through relationships between the employee base and management quickly deteriorated into toxicity as a result of a clash in corporate values, the lack of opportunities for promotion, and the employees' perception that their contributions were irrelevant (Maiorescu and Bendus 2011). Suicides in the workplace tend to occur among successful employees, who are generally overachievers and fully dedicated to their careers. Hence, the turmoil they experience in the workplace shatters their identity at its very core. Undoubtedly, they identify with the company and their work to a larger degree than the average employee. Hence, the discrepancy that emerges between a newly defined corporate identity that triggers toxicity in the workplace and the past one that had become an integral part of their own selves negatively impacts their well-being.

A classic example of a crisis that revolved around corporate identification took place at Disneyland in the 80s. In 1984, Disneyland employees engaged in a 22-day strike to protest management practices that were financially restrictive and that prioritized the bottom line over employee remuneration. In a seminal study published three years later, Smith and Eisenberg (1987) determined that the crisis arose as management and employees had divergent views of the company's values. Namely, for years, the company had been promoting the family metaphor according to which Disney was more than just a workplace: It was a family whose role and mission focused on providing happiness to other families. As the park underwent financial turmoil, management froze salaries, a step that the employees viewed as counter to the company's mission. They argued that families stick together in turbulent times and regarded the gesture as running contrary to what Walt Disney had envisioned. During the strike, the Disney employees held a vigil to honor founder Walt Disney and considered their protest an attempt to preserve his legacy. The following quote from interviews that Smith and Eisenberg (1987) conducted reflects employee sentiment:

It is not a strike over economics but policy and principle. It's the break of a family tradition; it's turning a family-oriented business into another cog of a large corporate structure and losing that identity. (376)

The strike ended when management obtained restraining orders, which led to the arrest of the union leaders and the dismissal of the employees (Smith and Eisenberg 1987). By taking these measures, management erased the interpretation of the family metaphor that was running contrary to the company's new orientation. By hiring new employees, Disney ensured that newcomers would be trained in the company's values in ways that aligned with the new mission. Apparently, management determined that it would be harder to shift current employees' perceptions of the family value orientation as opposed to hiring new employees who could easily embrace a new vision. Yet, the decision to release the employees involved in the strike meant that Disneyland lost those who had personally interacted with Walt Disney, who used to call him by his first name, and who had played a paramount role in shaping the company, its identity, and its internal culture. Some have observed that Disneyland has never been the same after the crisis because the internal culture that had been organically developed was erased and replaced with a post-Walt Disney one.

More recently, in 2022, Disney experienced an internal clash as the company took a stance on Florida's House Bill 1557, dubbed the "don't say gay" bill. The legislation, which restricts classroom discussions on sexual identity and orientation from kindergarten to grade three, triggered public criticism from the company while simultaneously alienating employees with opposing political views. More precisely, Disney employees who wanted the company to take a public stance against the bill regarded the CEO's response as slow, while employees who considered that their company should remain neutral felt silenced. The former protested against Disney and CEO Bob Chapek for not responding promptly, while the latter penned an unsigned letter that shed light on an internal culture of fear in which they felt pressured to hide their political views (Barrabi 2022; Reed 2022). The internal conflict could be assessed through the employees' divergent views of the company's community values. Disney defines community as the promotion of respect and understanding. The employees who wanted the company to be vocal about the legislation may have considered that it was imperative for Disney to engage in immediate advocacy against it out of respect for the LGBTQ+ community and in an attempt to foster respect for differences. By contrast, the employees who wanted their company to remain neutral may have viewed that state legislation did not fall under the purview of the entertainment industry and that fostering respect and understanding in communities should be done through the products and services that Disney offers.

The rift caused in Disney's internal culture likely persists to this day since internal cultures change slowly. However, no information is available to support this assumption. Disney's CEO Bob Chapek stepped down at the end of 2022 and Robert Iger, an executive with a long tenure with the company, took over. This leadership change could play a role in unifying Disney's workforce around a renewed vision that Mr. Iger may espouse and a definition of corporate values that delineates a clearer trajectory about the company's role in society. Nonetheless, employee interpretations of corporate values should be consistently assessed through internal surveys and by analysis of internal social media platforms. (Chapter 10 will provide details about the research methodologies used for this purpose.) Such analyses can shed light on divergent interpretations of corporate values that influence how employees identify with the company. If divergent perspectives are likely to cause a rift in the relationships that employees develop both with one another and with leadership, they should be promptly addressed at meetings, events, and employee forums. Leaders exert tremendous influence over the interpretation of corporate values. If they highlight the meaning they wish their employees to attribute to a corporate value, it is very likely that the employees will either adhere to this interpretation or leave the company if they disagree.

The present chapter detailed several internal crises. When companies face accidents, scandals, recalls, and the like, negative media coverage and the accusations that emerge online could lead to their employees feeling demoralized, which leads to low corporate identification. This low identification is demotivating and leads to low productivity, less effective problem-solving, and decreased creativity and innovation. Additionally, corporate identification itself can lead to crises as divergent interpretations of corporate values make companies unrecognizable in the eyes of their employees. During the stages of a crisis, it remains essential for communication professionals to constantly monitor employee views of the negative event and to request feedback to collectively manage the crisis. By valuing employee expertise and opinions, companies can not only address a crisis more efficiently but can solidify their employees' identification with the company. In cases in which the crisis itself emerges as a result of divergent interpretations of corporate values, a collective crisis management approach builds bridges across the company and unifies the employee base.

CHAPTER 5

Inclusion and Employee Engagement

The current chapter discusses the challenges that corporations face in their attempt to implement inclusive programs. It first tackles the prevalent top-down approach to diversity according to which management defines it and establishes diversity-centered programs. As an alternative, the chapter proposes an approach informed by the employees. Corporate employees represent their communities and are the ones who best understand the issues that they face. Further, by taking a bottom-up approach to inclusion, companies establish trust and foster open communication, which represents the precursors to successful relationship management and strong corporate identification.

Diversity and inclusion in corporations has been a topic widely researched across multiple fields and from a variety of angles. Researchers of organizational behavior, business studies, sociology, communication, and organizational psychology have extensively studied diversity in an attempt to understand how and why companies embrace differences. In terms of internal diversity, research has predominantly focused on the underrepresentation of minorities in the workplace (Applebaum, Walton, and Southerland 2015; Wallington 2024), what constitutes inclusive leadership (Mor Barak, Luria, and Brimhall 2022) and the impact of employee resource groups (ERGs) on fostering an inclusive internal culture (Jordan 2020; Lambert and Quintana 2015).

Scholars from the communication field have been particularly concerned about the fact that corporations embrace diversity from a business perspective and may focus predominantly on social issues that impact their bottom line. The concern emerged as scholars argued that by concentrating on causes that might generate profit, companies exert societal influence with respect to which diversity issues become more salient to the detriment of others. In other words, corporations define what diversity means, which groups are diverse, and what societal issues should be addressed over others (Vanhanen et al. 2023; Wrench 2005). Further, by extensively covering corporations, the media relays the salience of the diversity issues they embrace, leaving others aside. Therefore, the public becomes cognizant of social issues as defined by corporations and determined by their business interests while remaining unaware or oblivious to others. In this respect, media studies research showed that the importance that journalists attribute to an issue they cover transfers to the public (Wanta 2023). Specifically, news consumers perceive that certain issues take precedence over others depending on the frequency with which the media reports on them. Finally, scholars argued that by embracing diversity with a focus on the bottom line, companies encroach upon elected governments (Vanhanen et al. 2023; Wrench 2005), depriving citizens of voice.

The preceding business approach to diversity is known as diversity management and constitutes a top-down process through which management determines what diversity represents for the company, how it may benefit the organization, and how it should be implemented. Once defined in accordance with the mission statement and the corporation's values, diversity is implemented through the collaborations of several departments among which HR ensures the recruitment and retainment of diverse employees, ERGs aim to provide support and resources for specific minority groups, and internal communications assess the internal culture and address employee concerns. Despite these efforts, researchers found that corporate employees often display reticence toward diversity training and recruitment strategies, experiencing fatigue, anxiety, and fear (Dobbin and Kalev 2016; Kidder et al. 2004; Maiorescu-Murphy 2019). Moreover, employees tend to doubt their employers' intentions behind such programs, particularly as training meant to address differences seems to reinforce stereotypes and even lead to conflict and internal backlash (Bassett-Jones 2005; Dobbin and Kalev 2016; Kidder et al. 2004; Maiorescu-Murphy 2019; Schwabenland and Tomlinson 2015; Theodorakopoulos and Budhwar 2015).

Presently, corporate discrimination lawsuits continue to be on the rise (Society for Human Resource Management 2023). This raises questions about the need for improvements in employee relationships and engagement with leadership, all of which could lead to a positive and inclusive internal culture. For this purpose, communication scholarship proposed an employee approach to inclusion that should inform the development of programs from the bottom up. This approach will be discussed next in the context of the challenges that companies face internally as they currently embrace diversity predominantly through a top-down approach.

A Bottom-Up Approach to Inclusion

A main tenet of the business approach to diversity is the consideration that diversity increases creativity and innovation. Therefore, companies that rely heavily on research, such as the tech industry, the pharmaceutical sector, and the auto industry, have long focused on recruiting diverse employees to increase innovation. By contrast, research shows that in industries that revolve more around routine practices than creativity, such as the banking industry and the petroleum sector, companies focused on diversity projects less extensively in the past than they do today (Maiorescu-Murphy 2019; Maiorescu and Wrigley 2016). Since about 2020, as activists have put more pressure on corporations to adopt diversity practices, companies have implemented a larger number of diversity-centered projects aimed at their employees, consumers, and the communities in which they operate. Initially, corporations considered that these projects would showcase their commitment to society and foster relationships with consumers, activist groups, the media, and the government. However, companies that only recently have shown an interest in diversity have generally found it hard to develop relationships with their stakeholders (Maiorescu-Murphy 2022). In other words, consistency in diversity implementation proved paramount in convincing stakeholders that these efforts were genuine and not a response to a recent wave of activism (Maiorescu-Murphy 2022).

Recently, many corporations have stopped communicating to their public about diversity from a business perspective and have taken on a social responsibility approach to highlight their commitment to social causes. In previous years, when companies discussed their diversity programs, they argued that these initiatives both impacted the bottom line and aimed to address societal issues. Stakeholders often did not find corporate diversity initiatives entirely compelling. The few companies that still balanced business and societal contributions in their diversity discourses triggered a more positive reception (Maiorescu-Murphy 2022). This positive sentiment can be explained by the fact that, by delivering consistency, companies reinforced their identity and bolstered their stakeholders' identification with their values. Furthermore, this consistency has led the stakeholders to embrace specific messages related to diversity since to some degree these messages have fallen under their own system of values. It is important to remember that relationships between stakeholders and companies follow a similar path to the relationships we develop in everyday life. Consistent behavior is key to establishing trust and fostering a relationship. Conversely, inconsistent behavior leads us to doubt someone's reliability and sincerity and may erode trust.

Thus far, we have discussed several external reactions to corporate diversity programs. Next, let's switch our attention to what happens at an internal level and why employees may display diversity fatigue, fear, anxiety, and reticence, all of which can lead to turnover both in terms of minority employees and nonminority ones. Above all, despite their diversity-centered recruitment efforts, corporations oftentimes face reticence from diverse job applicants who avoid positions that stress the company's commitment to inclusion. For example, a study by Windscheid et al. (2017) found that female job applicants avoided job postings that encouraged women to apply for these positions and avowed the companies' commitment to bridging the gender gap. This begs the question of what could have gone wrong with the top-down business-centered approach to diversity.

First, corporations hired diverse employees that represented their consumer bases. For example, if a car company aimed to increase its sales in Hungary, the company needed employees of Hungarian origin to understand the market, the consumer culture, and to ultimately market, place, and sell its vehicles. Yet, one aspect that companies might have overlooked was the fact that recruitment was insufficient for diversity purposes and that retaining employees was a matter of building successful relationships across the company and ensuring a positive and inclusive internal culture. This short-sightedness is supported by research that looked at what leads to employee satisfaction and loyalty in the workplace. These studies show that minority employees want to feel empowered to contribute their unique expertise and to be regarded as an integral part of their company's success. Moreover, employee loyalty emerges as employees feel that they make a difference and have an impact on the operations and the overall success of their employer (Makhdoomi and Nika 2017).

According to identity theory (Burke and Stets 2022), an individual's identity encompasses multiple group memberships. Hence, an employee is a member of their company, a member of a specific ethnic group, a member of their family, and so on. The degree to which at any given time, an employee's membership plays more or less significant of a role is contingent upon the situation and the context they find themselves in. Hypothetically speaking, when a company like Google plans to develop new software and holds a meeting for this purpose, engineers who bring their expertise to the table may at that point identify with their profession or view themselves as members of their scientific community. Further, when managers ask them for specific input, the engineers may feel and view themselves as members of their company, while simultaneously identifying as members of their scientific community. Finally, if during the meeting, a minority engineer experiences what the literature refers to as a microaggression, their membership and affiliation to their ethnic community may take precedence over their identification with a scientific community or the company.

It can be argued that the shift in membership perceptions illustrates the constant individual need for belonging. Feeling that you belong to a community, that you are an integral part of your company and its success can make a difference between employee loyalty and turnover. This aspect is particularly important in the case of minority employees and women in male-dominated fields. Without a positive internal culture that genuinely embraces differences, employees may feel alienated and may experience difficulties building a solid internal network. Consequently, they might miss out on the resources and the information needed to navigate complex work-related situations and ascend to the corporate ladder (Downey et al. 2015; Ferraro, Hemsley, and Sands 2023). To prevent this, some corporations created ERGs dedicated to cultivating relationships among women and minority employees through workshops, training, and mentoring. Yet, research shows that while ERGs welcome nonminority employees, these seldom attend the groups' events; therefore, ERGs may not be as effective as expected at building collaborations and fostering relationships across a company. Additionally, women and minorities argued that by creating ERGs, companies signaled that diverse employees are in need of additional training and mentoring compared to their nonminority colleagues (Maiorescu and Wrigley 2016). Given these concerns, ERGs seem to best function as an auxiliary for inclusive programs rather than the exclusive solution to building an inclusive and welcoming internal culture (Lambert and Quintana 2015).

The current rise in the number of discrimination lawsuits in corporate America begs the question of what happens after the recruitment process is completed. Specifically, what is the workplace atmosphere like that leads to turnover and discrimination lawsuits? In research from business and organizational studies, scholars coined the term organizational justice (Park and Kim 2023; Sumarjo, Haerofiatna, and Haryadi 2024) to refer to the fact that employees expect equal treatment in terms of compensation, benefits, and opportunities for promotion. Additionally, employees expect that rules apply evenly across the employee base, including repercussions and demotions. Consequently, if rules and compensation apply evenly, the internal culture remains one aspect of the corporate life that should ensure that every employee feels valued for their expertise, their differences, and the enhanced contributions they can bring to their company. Moreover, an inclusive internal culture fosters relationships among employees and gives everyone formal and informal access to valuable information regarding promotion opportunities, problem-solving, and mentoring.

Such a culture could be triggered through a bottom-up approach to diversity, as discussed next.

By fostering relationships among employees and between employees and leadership, companies cultivate a context conducive to the organic development of inclusion and the appreciation for differences. Namely, if leadership cultivates quality relationships with their employees and encourages the development of a positive internal culture, inclusion emerges organically as employees appreciate one another for their diverse backgrounds, expertise, and increased creativity and innovation.

As discussed in the previous chapters, companies recruit employees based on the degree to which they identify with the company's values and mission. Therefore, upon recruitment, employees already identify with their company to a certain degree. The identification increases when corporations foster a positive internal culture that gives the employees a sense of belonging. This culture addresses the impediments that minority employees may face in the workplace, such as alienation, the lack of a solid network, mentorship, and valuable information. An inclusive internal culture represents the consequence of solid relationships built across the employee base through a continued communication flow within and across departments. Communication scholars emphasize the importance of public relations practitioners playing an integral role in fostering diversity in the workplace. Through event planning, social media communication, and employee engagement, PR practitioners can foster bonds across the employee base, therefore setting the tone for relationship building. Finally, through annual employee surveys and by scanning internal social media platforms, PR professionals can detect and address issues related to diversity and bring them to the management's attention. For example, communication on internal social media channels can shed light on whether employees feel comfortable in the workplace and have access to the resources and the information they need.

Research from business studies and communication has discussed the concept of tokenism extensively (Drenten, Harrison, and Pendarvis 2023) along with its impact on employee morale. Tokenism may occur in various settings, ranging from women and minority employees perceiving that their company hired them to meet the requirements of affirmative action, to being asked to contribute their expertise only as it pertains to understanding their specific communities. Undoubtedly, perceived tokenism lowers corporate identification as employees do not feel appreciated for their experience beyond that which pertains to the understanding of diverse issues. The bottom-up approach to diversity has the potential to avert tokenism as it implies that both minority and nonminority employees contribute to a company's diversity efforts. Specifically, the approach involves constant feedback from across the employee base with respect to societal issues that the employees regard as paramount for the communities in which their company operates (Maiorescu-Murphy 2019).

Undoubtedly, minority employees' unique perspectives and knowledge of societal issues can inform relevant programs as to how the company can engage internally and externally. Yet, collectively, all the employees can participate in such programs, which in turn strengthens the relationships among employees along with their identification with the company. Specifically, if a conversation between leaders and employees leads to the implementation of a program through which employees will visit middle schoolers in the area to advise on STEM careers, the involvement of all the employees strengthens relationships across the company. Moreover, this involvement bolsters their identification with the company given that the participating employees get involved in a program that aligns with their own values, beliefs, and passions. A company needs a multitude of similar diversity programs that are developed and implemented through employee engagement and feedback. This variety appeals to a wider range of employees and interests and, consequently, has the potential to lead to higher employee engagement. There is no doubt that diversity implemented through a bottom-up approach will impact the bottom line. Yet, its impact is indirect, long-term, and falls under the umbrella of corporate social responsibility (CSR). As a company consistently contributes to the communities in which it operates, it builds or adds to an already established positive reputation. Research shows that CSR and a positive reputation enable companies to recruit the most talented job applicants and trigger both employee and consumer loyalty (Maiorescu and Wrigley 2016; Min, Kim, and Yang 2023).

The important role that transformational leadership plays in employee engagement in inclusion cannot be overstated, and diversity programs represent an opportunity for leaders to incorporate their employees' vision into their own. Past studies pointed out that previously developed high-quality relationships between leaders and employees lead to increased engagement of employees in CSR programs in general (Mallory and Rupp 2014) and those related to diversity in particular (Hong and Ji 2022). In addition, by taking an active part in the development and implementation of projects that appeal to their own interests and values, employees learn to appreciate differences as they gain a deeper understanding of the societal issues that communities face. This participation in community/diversity programs which oftentimes takes place outside the workplace represents an opportunity for learning, fostering bonds across the employee base, and leading to the elimination of bias.

To promote this bottom-up approach, corporations should make extensive use of their internal social media platforms to create online communities. First, employees (particularly newcomers) will join an online community as a result of what the literature refers to as identity-based attachment (Kwon and Sejin 2023) or, in this case, corporate identification. In time, increased and recurrent online interactions are likely to lead to bonds among employees that have the potential to translate into offline interactions. Research indicates that engaging in online communication may reduce stereotyping and bias (Maiorescu-Murphy 2019): In an online environment, employees may bond with more ease as they communicate around their commonalities. In time, the relationships formed online translate into face-to-face interactions. The fact that the bond was formed in a context void of social markers and around similar interests is likely to make relationships more durable and solid. Because an internal online community implies recurrent social media interactions, it ensures a continuous information flow for support and mentorship.

Further, the very content users produce in online communities can inform the company about which social issues minority employees consider important for their company to address. This valuable input can give insight into the support that such projects may receive across the employee base. Next, an online community provides an opportunity for the communication department to trigger dialogue around diversity and to directly ask employees what projects the company might consider in the future. Finally, the user-generated content can shed light on potential issues related to diversity that are present in the internal culture. Online users in general reveal more about themselves online than they do in offline settings. Online self-disclosure tends to be higher because, in a virtual environment, users never fully grasp the entirety of the audience that their posts will reach. Hence, discussions on internal social media platforms can bring to light significant issues in the internal culture that employees face that can be addressed before they turn into crises, turnover, and future litigation. By addressing these issues, a company takes a proactive step toward inclusivity and showcases commitment.

Oftentimes companies believe that their internal social media platforms represent online communities. Yet, what characterizes an online community goes beyond a high number of followers and increased online interactions around sporadic corporate posts. An online community implies recurrent online interactions whether these are at times high or low. Hence, the quality of these interactions is important and quality implies ongoing online communication. Recurrent users are the ones who establish close bonds with one another and who organically emerge as leaders on their company's platform. To trigger recurrent interactions, public relations practitioners should focus on what drives employees to communicate online with their company. As previously discussed, generally, it is corporate identification. Consequently, some of the corporate posts should revolve around the company's values. Next, employees need access to information that is relevant to their positions, assignments, and departments. Finally, posts should entail some casual information that is not necessarily related to the company. After all, casual conversations remain the very purpose of social media communication. Building online communities represents a tedious task. With time and persistence, its benefits, including relationship management and enhanced corporate identification, can trigger the development of diversity programs that lead to increased employee loyalty and the retention of minority employees, while making an external impact on society and adding to a company's positive reputation.

The present chapter discussed several challenges that corporations face as they frame inclusion from a top-down approach. It proposed that corporations engage their employees in determining diversity programs that they themselves create and that align with a company's values. It is important to note that this chapter does not argue for the adoption of an exclusive bottom-up approach to diversity. Corporations can balance their top-down approach with a bottom-up one. However, for diversity initiatives to be truly impactful, the vast majority of them should be developed with the help of those employees who face social issues in everyday life, including in the workplace. For this purpose, the chapter discussed the use of online and offline communication to foster relationship management, corporate identification, and diversity.

PART 2

External Communication

CHAPTER 6

Relationships With Consumers

The present chapter focuses on developing and maintaining relationships with external stakeholder groups. It pays particular attention to the way corporations foster these relationships via corporate identification in online and offline environments. In addition, the chapter introduces the tenets of a communication theory that can foster relationships on social media via dialogue. As a practical application, the reader will be exposed to Wendy's relationship management strategy.

Successful Customer Relationship Management

Wendy's continued success is not only the result of its products but also a direct consequence of the consistency with which the company has promoted its identity and values in the experiences it delivers to consumers. From its joyful logo, inspired by the founder's daughter, to its store designs and marketing campaigns, Wendy's delivers an experience of warmth and coziness reflective of its values among which are transparency and responsibility. The values themselves represent two major ingredients of successful relationships. Without transparency and responsibility in one's communication and actions, trust cannot be established. Without trust, relationships cannot develop. Other values that form Wendy's identity, including respect, fair treatment, and equality, constitute additional precursors to relationship development and management. Undoubtedly, no relationship can develop without respect and the fair treatment of the parties involved. Similar to transparency and responsibility, respect, equality, and fair treatment enable the company to gain the trust of its consumers. Positive purchasing/dining experiences further bolster through the consistent implementation of these values. The warmth and coziness of Wendy's stores decrease the power distance between a large corporate conglomerate and provide a family-like atmosphere that connotes equal treatment.

In addition to positively projecting its corporate values in its stores, Wendy's is known for its successful social media presence that, as of February 2024, involves 8.4 million followers on Facebook, 3.8 million on X, and 1.1 million followers on Instagram. It would be almost impossible to find a Gen Z representative who is unfamiliar with Wendy's online humor and witty remarks. Through its social media communication, the company further promotes its values, making the brand recognizable for its warmth, respect, and transparency as Wendy's has embraced a casual and transparent tone. Above all, the extensive social media communication that the company engages in reflects a penchant for transparency, as the more corporations engage their consumers in online environments, the more they risk receiving negative comments. Therefore, by extensively communicating online, Wendy's demonstrates vulnerability, an essential element of relationship management. The consistency with which the company promotes its values across offline and online platforms leads to the development of corporate identification, as (potential) consumers understand the brand and what it stands for. Moreover, the brand delivers its values across multiple marketing communication functions among which are sales, marketing, advertising, and public relations (social media communication).

In time, Wendy's consistency translates into reliability as the brand becomes recognizable for its warmth, transparency, coziness, and fair treatment. Therefore, a one-time consumer may start to trust the company and identify with at least some of its values. This initial identification leads to the establishment of a relationship with the company that Wendy's maintains through its consistent promotion of values. As touched upon in the previous chapters, such values are ambiguously defined in order to facilitate the identification of a large spectrum of consumers. For example, each of us may attribute a different connotation to respect, yet each of us appreciates the value of respect.

It can be argued that the relationship between (potential) consumers and a company starts when the consumers display corporate identification. Next, companies continue to maintain the relationship via traditional and new communication channels that they use to strengthen identification. In a highly competitive market that abounds in choice, it is the relationship that has been developed and maintained that leads consumers to prefer a specific company over its competitors.

To successfully develop and maintain relationships, companies must mimic the communication practices that lead to healthy relationships in everyday life. Specifically, relationships cannot exist outside communication processes whether these are verbal or nonverbal. Furthermore, in the case of an already established relationship, the lack of constant communication erodes trust and can actually lead to the demise of the relationship. For example, a company that does not update its social media accounts regularly or does not respond to user complaints may give the impression of a lack of professionalism, a lack of care for its consumers, and possibly disrespect, all of which run contrary to the company's value of putting consumers first.

However, constant communication may be inefficient if void of quality. In our daily lives, we use a combination of one-way communication (information giving) and two-way communication (dialogue). Since successful relationships revolve around respect, then our engagement with each other should involve a blend of information giving, active listening, and responding to meet each other's needs. Before the advent of Web 2.0, corporations had to invest significant resources into receiving consumer feedback. Much of this feedback represented the result of strenuous research conducted through surveys, focus groups, and interviews that companies learned from in order to deliver quality products and services inspired by consumer needs and expectations. The delivery of such products and services represented a company's way of telling consumers that they listened. By contrast, today social media engagement represents an instant means to receive and respond to feedback. Corporations make extensive use of extensive consumer data to assess changes in marketing needs and consumer behavior. The ultimate purpose is to deliver what consumers expect and to even exceed their expectations. Social media communication represents a way through which companies trigger consumer feedback while simultaneously bolstering identification with their values.

Unfortunately, companies make predominant use of one-way communication as they inform their followers on a variety of topics that range from operations to products, services, and CSR. The prevalent one-way communication is not effective at triggering responses that inform a company's marketing functions. The lack of dialogic communication, which implies a constant feedback loop, deprives companies of opportunities to further build on the relationships developed through corporate identification. Several research studies on corporate social media engagement have pointed out the opportunities that companies miss as they predominantly engage in one-way social media communication (Aichner 2021; Okazaki 2020).

It is for this purpose that the next section will focus on how companies can build dialogue online and discuss a prevalent communication theory along with its practical applications.

Social Media and Consumer Relationships

Corporations have successfully embraced social media platforms by adapting their casual tone and communication style. The features of social media platforms mirror their initial purpose: to get in touch and stay in touch. At first, many online users viewed the very presence of corporations on social media as an inappropriate intrusion. Yet, by adopting a friendly communication style and by focusing to a larger degree on casual topics rather than marketing messages, companies not only justified their social media presence but also managed to draw a significant number of followers and user-generated content. Web 2.0 era engendered the empowerment of online users, and hence the consumers, who have become cognizant of the influence they exert on corporations so long as they enjoy a robust network. They expect to be valued and recognized for their online contributions as evident in the number of times the general user checks the likes, reposts, and comments on posts they've received (Figure 6.1).

Dimension	Explanation	Example
Mutuality	Seek collaborations with consumers	"What else do you expect from our products/services?"
Propinquity	Seek input into decision-making	"Name one program that your neighborhood needs!"
Empathy	Offer continual support	"Facing midterms? Share 5 tips to survive them! The first 20 users who respond will receive a $10 gift card."
Risk	Respond to online backlash and perceived failure)	"We are sorry. Let us make it up to you."
Commitment	Constantly incorporate online consumer feedback	"We'll look into how this product can be improved in the future. We will be back in touch."

Figure 6.1 The dialogic theory, (Kent and Taylor 2002)

The framework that has been widely used to generate online engagement represents the dialogic theory of public relations (Kent and Taylor 2002; Kent 2023; Sommerfeldt and Yang 2018).

The application of theory in the industry has the potential to strengthen a company's relationships with its stakeholders online. The dialogic theory revolves around five principles that will be detailed next: mutuality, propinquity, empathy, risk, and commitment (Kent and Taylor 2002; Kent 2023; Sommerfeldt and Yang 2018). First, mutuality refers to a company's attempt at seeking collaborations with its consumers. For example, contrary to simply delivering a new product based on marketing research, companies could regularly ask their social media followers what they are expecting from a specific product. By doing so, companies not only stay up to date with the latest consumer expectations but also appeal to the social media users' need for empowerment and validation. Consequently, certain corporate products and services will derive from a collaborative approach rather than a top-down decision-making process.

The second dimension of the dialogic theory is propinquity which refers to the fact that true dialogue requires input into decision making. For instance, corporations have long developed CSR projects by taking a managerial approach to ensure that their efforts not only helped communities but also impacted the bottom line. Embracing propinquity would mean that companies oftentimes consult with their consumers on projects that they consider beneficial for their communities. In a nutshell, to some degree, the consumer would enjoy decision-making powers. To provide a concrete example, companies could ask their followers: "What would be a program that you consider that your community/neighborhood needs?" To increase the likelihood of online interactions and responses, communication professionals may consider a contest and offer economic rewards to the first 20 users who offer their feedback. The contest is likely to trigger an even higher number of responses when it considers social rewards in addition to economic ones (gift cards, free subscriptions, etc.). The social rewards occur when companies respond to the feedback they have received through likes, comments, and shares, all of which lead online users to experience self-efficacy. By experiencing self-efficacy, users feel an integral part of the company which may strengthen their corporate identification.

As for the economic awards, practitioners should consider the fact that the value of such awards is less significant than the gesture itself. More precisely, whether a company gives away $5 gift cards or $15 ones is unlikely to make a difference in terms of online interactions. Both $5 gift cards and $15 ones create a sense of urgency to respond and engender excitement around the competition. Finally, "winning" the competition and being acknowledged by a company through comments, shares, or likes increases the users' status within their own social media network and helps consumers gain recognition among their online peers.

Empathy constitutes the third dialogic dimension and is extant when corporations offer continual support and their efforts lead to the creation of a communal mindset. Specifically, by supporting their consumers and by attempting to work collectively to solve problems, companies and consumers find themselves in a mutually beneficial relationship. This relationship is one of problem-solving: the company needs to sell a product and the consumers buy it to satisfy a need. Support is a term with many connotations. On the one hand, it can refer to customer issues that companies continuously solve on social media. Addressing them in a public forum increases trust and signifies transparency. Support may additionally refer to issues outside the business realm. For example, one of Wendy's followers makes the following comment: "I have two midterms this week. Can I get a free burger if I score an A in both?" An empathetic reply could read:

"OMG we remember those days. DM us and we'll send you a gift card." Moreover, Wendy's could create a post offering five-dollar gift cards to the first 20 users who share how their midterms are going. An example of such a post would be: "Facing midterms? We are cheering for you! Share 2 tips for unwinding during midterms. We will reward the first 20 users who respond with a $5 gift card they can use at any Wendy's location." This competition displays empathy, creates dialogue, increases interactivity, and fosters relationships.

Risk represents the fourth dimension of dialogue. There is an indisputable degree of risk in any online interaction, and it is mostly risk that precludes companies from engaging their consumers in genuine dialogue. The more companies expose their products, services, and operations, the more they ask for feedback in an attempt to create a consumer-company collaboration, and the more they potentially open the door to negative feedback that could go viral. The importance of risk cannot be overstated and there is no better department to remind us of it than the legal one. Yet, as is the case with our own interpersonal interactions, risk denotes vulnerability and vulnerability increases trust, strengthens a relationship, and fosters deeper identification between the interlocutors.

There are various examples that have shown us that risk and vulnerability can lead to improved operations and corporate policies. For example, in 2018, T-Mobile Australia changed its policies to secure customer passwords after an exchange on X (former Twitter) between a company representative and a customer revealed that T-Mobile was saving passwords in clear text. In a response to a customer that denotes the transparency imposed by a true commitment to dialogue, a T-Mobile representative wrote: "Customer service could see part of each password. … We secure all data very carefully, so there is not a thing to fear" (Griffith 2018). Promptly after this revelation, T-Mobile tweeted that it would revise its policies, which it did. This revelation, while potentially very risky for T-Mobile, led to the improvement of its policies and enhanced consumer data protection. Above all, by occurring in a public forum, the transparency of the representative and the promptness of policy change increased consumer trust. It is important to note that consumers have shown over and over again that they are less concerned about mistakes that companies make and more focused on how companies address them.

Finally, commitment represents the remaining dimension espoused in the dialogic theory and refers to a company's dedication to actively listening to and accepting opposing views. The dimension implies that companies committed to dialogue would attempt to find common ground. In practice, there is a myriad of instances in which social media users critiqued corporations, their products, and their operations. While approximately two-thirds of social media complaints revolve around product-related issues, a third of the negative comments refer to corporate operations such as employee compensation, CSR, and sustainability. By actively listening to consumers and being willing to find common ground, companies adapt to the ever-changing expectations of the macroenvironment in which they operate while strengthening relationships with not only potential and existing consumers but also with activist groups and journalists.

While the dialogic theory has been predominantly applied in research studies conducted on online platforms, it is also applicable offline. In both online and offline environments, dialogue represents an ongoing process with a back-and-forth conversation that involves risk, commitment, asking for the interlocutor's feedback, and incorporating it to adapt to their needs.

In offline settings, such as stores, the sales force represents the face of the corporation, and their interpersonal communication skills, whether verbal or nonverbal, can transform a consumer's corporate identification into a long-term corporate-consumer relationship. Moreover, the feedback received from consumers can inform marketing practices, while critiques and issues can be addressed in-store. Addressing such issues leads to satisfied consumers who spread positive word-of-mouth, the most influential marketing strategy to date. Decades of research show that satisfied consumers share about their experience with up to three friends while dissatisfied ones with eight. Of course, online, the power of a consumer is amplified by a large network. Further, a consumer whose issue is addressed is three times more likely to be loyal to a company than a consumer who has never experienced problems. Above all, active listening itself may suffice in circumstances where companies cannot solve certain customer issues. Oftentimes, frustrated consumers understand that the company cannot address their issues, yet remain recurrent customers because either at the store, or by phone, through chat, or on social media, the company listened attentively and engaged in a meaningful dialogue.

Online, corporations attempt to engage in dialogue by asking pertinent questions related to their operations and products. Despite the increased number of responses they may get, companies seldom follow through. In this case, the communication attempt is perceived as faux-dialogue or what the literature refers to as two-way asymmetrical communication (Grunig and Grunig 2013). It is possible that a company genuinely uses online responses to address issues in its products and operations. However, without making its decisions known to its followers, these efforts lead to perceptions of impression management as opposed to commitment to dialogue. By contrast, if companies respond to social media suggestions, issues, and feedback, they engage in genuine dialogue or two-way symmetrical communication (Grunig and Grunig 2013). It would be impossible for a company to provide a solution to every issue that customers bring or to take into account all the external perspectives regarding its operations. However, stakeholders are oftentimes looking for an explanation for a corporate decision that does not address their needs. For example, when a company asks its online followers about possible CSR projects they think the company should embrace, communication practitioners should assess the responses and relay them to upper management. The data must be analyzed in terms of the frequency of similar proposals and the impact of such projects on communities and the company. Once the company reaches a decision, communication practitioners should follow up on the social media discussion to express thanks for the suggestions and to inform the online users on what projects will be addressed, why, and what their impact is expected to be. More importantly, practitioners should provide reasons as to why other proposals could not come to fruition at this time and whether the company may reconsider them in the future. This step validates online users, showcases transparency and commitment to dialogue, and fosters relationships. Finally, it increases the visibility and the online status of the users the company interacts with and may lead to future relationships with the users' own network.

There are several additional considerations with respect to the application of the dialogic theory. The dimensions intertwine and overlap and companies should adopt mutuality, propinquity, empathy, risk, and commitment to their values. For example, risk differs across industries and from company to company. Therefore, when implementing the dialogic theory, communication professionals should define what each dimension means for their company. Specifically, with respect to commitment, the communication team may ask: "How do we show commitment to social media dialogue in a way that reflects our corporate values?" Another important consideration is that companies often use questions that sound more rhetorical than engaging and ultimately lead to less interactivity than anticipated. To avert this, communication professionals should ensure that their questions give followers a sense of urgency that triggers them to respond the moment they read the post. Consider the following example: "What's the first thing you'll do when spring arrives? Can we get 50 ideas in 5 minutes?"

This chapter looked at the importance of dialogue in maintaining relationships with external stakeholder groups. While it focuses predominantly on consumers, companies can apply the principles of dialogic theory as they build relationships with other external stakeholders, including activist groups. These principles are particularly effective on social media platforms where corporate transparency constitutes the sine qua non for successful interactivity. An important consideration is that by enacting the dialogic dimensions, companies can not only foster consumer relationships but also contribute to building social capital. It could be argued that dialogue inadvertently enables companies to create one of their most significant CSR projects. Specifically, past research has shown that while offline interactions are often insufficient to create close bonds within and across neighborhoods, online interaction around a common interest (in this case, a company) can lead in time to close bonds among users. Such close bonds trigger the formation of an online community around the company whose interactions possibly go beyond brand-related conversations to include topics of everyday life. This close-knit community is likely to draw on its collective resources (social capital) to help its members with issues that range from minor to severe, including crises (Maiorescu-Murphy 2019). Thus, by triggering dialogue, companies can not only benefit themselves but society at large.

CHAPTER 7

Global and International Relationship Management

Multinational corporations must build relationships with their stakeholders worldwide, which can be challenging given the differences across international milieus. This chapter will discuss the environmental variables that affect the success of efforts that corporations make to effectively build relationships: political economy, media system, culture, and the level of activism. Next, it will discuss the differences between an international versus a global approach to relationship management by looking at IKEA's and Nike's social media presence. Finally, the chapter will discuss building relationships abroad through the application of cultural dimensions and the psychology of colors.

Global Relationship Management

IKEA's Instagram presence sheds light on a communication strategy meant to build relationships in several geographic environments in which the company has a significant number of consumers, including Kuwait, Poland, the Dominican Republic, and the United States. Specifically, IKEA dedicates an Instagram account for each of the preceding countries and tailors its online communication to be culture-specific. By taking this approach, known in research as global communication, IKEA is able to adapt its values to meet different cultural expectations (Johnston 2020; Verčič and Sriramesh 2019). Strategic ambiguity is a concept discussed in previous chapters with respect to its role in facilitating the identification of a wide range of company stakeholders. This concept is particularly important in the context of global communication. When companies build relationships with their consumers abroad, the ambiguity of their values allows them to promote their identity by slightly shifting their meaning and connotations to suit an international environment. For example, one of IKEA's values represents togetherness, which the company defines as trusting one another to take the same path. While all cultures value togetherness and family, differences do exist in the degree to which societies are community-oriented (collective) versus individual-oriented (individualistic). Therefore, an effective way to promote togetherness can be accomplished through visuals that depict not only family members but also co-workers and neighbors for collective cultures while predominantly posting about family in individualistic countries.

Corporations often adapt to their audiences abroad by emphasizing certain values while downplaying others. Specifically, sustainability is an additional value that IKEA holds. This value is likely to emerge differently, depending on the economic development of a country. More precisely, countries with a robust economic system enjoy more resources that they can allocate toward sustainable projects and generally exhibit higher levels of consumer activism and awareness. By contrast, developing economies face significant challenges and may have to prioritize funding health care and education over sustainable projects. Undoubtedly, this does not imply that the citizens of the developing world do not value sustainability. Rather, it signals the fact that citizens may face daily economic challenges that prevent them from making sustainability a top priority. Given these cultural differences, companies may promote their value of sustainability to a greater degree in developed countries compared to developing ones. For example, in the case of developing economies, IKEA may decide to focus on another core corporate value, namely cost-consciousness. By emphasizing this value over others, IKEA can foster relationships by adapting to consumers' needs for quality yet accessible products.

Thus far, we have discussed the corporate adaptation to different countries via two strategies: ambiguity and the emphasis on a certain value over others. Yet, what do companies take into account when they decide how to adapt to international environments? According to research in communication management, corporations should take into account certain environmental variables, including political economy, the media, the level of activism, and the culture, all of which exert influence on how companies promote their values, foster identification, and build relationships (Verčič and Sriramesh 2019). For the purpose of brevity and clarity, political systems can be classified as democracies (in which several political parties and political figures compete in free elections), authoritarian regimes (governed by one party or the military), and monarchies. Furthermore, monarchies may be traditional (in which the monarch or the royal family holds the absolute power) and constitutional monarchies (characterized by limited monarchal power and much of the responsibility delegated to elected bodies). The existing political system exerts influence on additional environmental variables such as activism and the media system. For example, the media are free from censorship in democracies and government-controlled under authoritarian regimes. While democracies promote freedom of speech and, consequently, activism, such activities are nonexistent under authoritarian regimes.

By far the most complex environmental variable is culture, for which scholars have identified over 1,000 definitions (Sriramesh 2012). Both theoreticians and practitioners have extensively relied on the work of Dutch social psychologist Geert Hofstede (2011), whose cultural dimensions enabled companies to successfully adapt on a global level. The cultural dimensions that Hofstede proposed include power distance, individualism, motivation for success, uncertainty avoidance, long-term orientation, and indulgence (Hofstede 2011; Khan, Varaksina, and Hinterhuber 2024; Matharu 2024). To assess these dimensions, practitioners can use The Country Comparison Tool provided by the Culture Factor Group. The comparison tool can be accessed at https://www.hofstede-insights.com/country-comparison-tool and provides a graphic representation along with explanations for each variable of a chosen country.

First, power distance refers to the degree to which the citizens of a country expect that power would be distributed equally across organizations and societies. Democratic countries are lower in power distance compared to societies governed by authoritarian regimes and monarchies. Significant discrepancies exist particularly when the comparison involves a more religious or spiritual society. For example, on a scale from 1 to 100, the United States scores 40 on power distance while Kuwait 90. To refer back to IKEA, the company can expect that its followers from Kuwait would engage online to a lesser extent than those in the United States. This represents a consequence of the fact that users from countries high on power distance generally may perceive IKEA as a giant conglomerate they should contact for customer service purposes rather than inconsequential and informal conversations.

Second, the dimension of individualism refers to the degree to which a culture promotes individuality versus group memberships. In other words, do people view themselves as part of a community, a collective, or as individuals who have to be independent enough to cater to their own needs? The United States scores 60 on individualism while Kuwait's score is 28. The score implies that IKEA may have an easier time facilitating corporate identification with consumers in Kuwait due to their penchant to view themselves as members of a group. A caveat represents the fact that the high power distance that characterizes the Kuwaiti culture may prevent online users from engaging in constant interactions with the company, impeding its efforts to build an online community that would cement group membership.

It is important to note that the dimension of collectivism is conducive to effective internal relationships, as corporations that operate in countries high on collectivism have an easier time building a positive internal culture that bolsters employee identification with the company. Namely, IKEA may have an easier time retaining its employees based in Kuwait because they view themselves as members of their team and may prefer to continue to support their colleagues rather than leave. Additionally, providing a sense of belonging represents an integral part of IKEA's identity, as displayed in its values of togetherness and caring for people. The company can more easily facilitate corporate identification and cultivate a family environment in collective cultures. By contrast, the American culture is more dynamic, and its emphasis on individuality means that employees are not hesitant to leave a company when a better career opportunity arises.

Third, the Culture Factor Group refers to the drive toward success as an indication of whether the citizens of a country are motivated by high competitiveness, achievement, and a desire to become number one. A lower score is not an indication that people do not value success; rather, it shows that they are more motivated by different factors such as quality of life and concern for others. The United States scores 60 on this dimension and Kuwait 40. These scores imply that IKEA would be successful in promoting online competitions to its followers in the United States, which is an effective means to promote increased online engagement and foster identification with the company. Yet, competitive tactics used on its Kuwaiti account may not render similar positive results.

Fourth, the dimension of uncertainty avoidance enables companies to get a grasp on the degree to which a society tolerates ambiguity, unknown situations, and an uncertain future. The United States scores 48 on uncertainty avoidance, compared to Kuwait whose score is 80. This dimension is essential for communication practices aimed at building both internal and external relationships. For example, IKEA has to communicate more precisely in Kuwait than in the United States to avoid a possible misinterpretation of its messages. In the case of a product recall, it is expected that consumers from countries high on uncertainty avoidance, such as Kuwait, would try to make sense of the situation and engage in more suppositions should the company not update them promptly. As users try to make sense of the situation online, rumors can quickly become viral and escalate into a greater crisis, causing significant damage to corporate reputation. Social media has significantly reduced the time span that corporations have to address consumer concerns before they become crises. Yet, in countries high on uncertainty avoidance, consumers not only expect a quicker explanation of a crisis or a concern, but they also expect enhanced clarity. Such cultures are high in context and have communication practices that imply reading between the lines, inferring meaning, and attributing connotations to a larger extent than countries low on uncertainty avoidance.

Social media increases the likelihood of misinterpretations as a result of the lack of nonverbal communication, including body language, gestures, pitch, tone, voice, and so on. However, companies can reduce possible misinterpretations by combining text with visuals (videos and/or photos) to ensure the delivery of nonverbal communication. For example, in the case of a response to a product recall, corporations could post a video of their CEO addressing the crisis in addition to the text that discusses the details of the process.

Internally, employees in cultures high on uncertainty avoidance value high-quality relationships with leaders. From the perspective of the leader-member exchange theory discussed in previous chapters, high-quality relationships promote not only material exchanges but also social and emotional ones. Emotional and social rewards and high-quality relationships with managers provide employees from countries high on uncertainty avoidance with job security, which, in turn, motivates them to achieve more and strengthens their identification with the company and the employee base.

Fifth, the dimension of long-term orientation enables companies to understand cultures by determining the extent to which they balance change with traditions. Specifically, the dimension refers to whether a society is oriented more toward the future or if it embraces its norms and traditions from the past. The United States scores 50 on long-term orientation while Kuwait 30. Let's assume that to promote corporate identification, IKEA would have to adapt its value of simplicity to both the American and the Kuwaiti environments. Given that the United States is higher on long-term orientation, consumers may be more inclined to try out new products despite the fact that these may not align with their past preferences. By contrast, in Kuwait, IKEA would need to deliver simplicity by connecting its furniture designs to those that its potential consumers are familiar with.

Finally, the sixth dimension constitutes indulgence or the degree to which a society feels free or constrained by social norms and expectations. This dimension is calculated by looking at a variety of factors that range from enjoying leisure time to spending on products and services. The United States scores 68 on indulgence, while Arab countries such as Kuwait score an average of 22. In practice, these results suggest that IKEA's social media communication should reflect the company's values in visual contexts that depict pastime and leisure activities more in the United States than in Kuwait. To promote its value of simplicity, IKEA could provide an illustration of a simplistic interior design on its Kuwaiti account and an indoor get-together before a sports event in the United States.

Not all of Hofstede's cultural dimensions apply to a specific corporate situation. Depending on what a company decides to focus on (e.g., employee relationships, consumer relationships, etc.), practitioners can choose the dimension(s) that best suit their purpose. For example, if a company faces a crisis, the dimension of indulgence is less relevant in a response compared to the dimension of uncertainty avoidance.

Further, to effectively address corporate identification globally, companies can promote their values by making use of the psychology of colors. Colors trigger emotions and feelings and can make a corporate message memorable (Kim et al. 2024; Pichierri and Pino 2023; Singh and Srivastava 2011). A simple online search for "the meaning of colors" reveals the symbolism and meanings behind the colors on the spectrum that enable practitioners to be persuasive. For example, IKEA's logo is depicted in blue and yellow. Blue denotes trust and tranquility, while yellow conveys energy, youth, vibrancy, and happiness. Consequently, the color behind the logo accurately represents the company's values, including togetherness, caring for people, and taking responsibility. Undoubtedly, a company doesn't need to regularly use its logo colors in its social media communication. Other colors may effectively represent the corporate values, such as orange, which denotes vitality and energy, and brown, which connotes reliability. Through a combination of photos/videos, colors, and text that converge to denote corporate values, companies are more effective at delivering a consistent identity. Further, a consistent identity is essential for establishing and maintaining stakeholder trust and identification with the company.

The psychology of colors can be adapted to different business environments where a global approach is important. Hofstede's cultural dimensions are particularly useful for this purpose. For example, in a culture high in power distance and low in long-term orientation, such as Kuwait, IKEA can convey its values of togetherness and caring for people through social media posts that predominantly use brown color. The use of the color brown conveys honesty and reliability, both of which relate to IKEA's values. Above all, using brown facilitates adaptation to Kuwaiti culture, as the color also conveys conservatism. In sum, the combination of Hofstede's cultural dimensions and the psychology of colors enables companies to adapt their values and identity across international environments. However, there are cases where companies choose not to adapt their communication practices to specific international environments. Rather, they prefer to adopt a one-size-fits-all approach known as international communication, as discussed next.

International Relationship Management

An effective way to illustrate the one-size-fits-all approach is illustrated by Nike's presence on Instagram. The company has several different accounts, including Nike running, Nike football (soccer), and Nike basketball, to name a few. Contrary to IKEA's adaptation to various countries of operations, Nike took an international approach and focused on building online communities around two interests: a specific sport and its brand. Research has shown that people join communities around an interest that may range from sports and social activity to health and politics (Sison 2017). Their passion for the issue drives increased online interactions, closer bonds among community members, and an enhanced commitment to contributing content online. Consequently, Nike's followers identify with the company and its values and, additionally, share a passion for a specific sport, both of which encourage social media interactions that further bolster the users' identification with the company. Yet, Nike's online followers hail from across the world and one would wonder how the company can maintain relationships online and communicate to meet multicultural expectations. Research shows that when online users have a strong passion for an issue, they form their own online culture (Schembri and Latimer 2016; Sison 2017). Specifically, through constant interactions, they bring their diverse perspectives, interests, and communication styles into continued conversations that, in time, morph into a cyberculture. The culture entails its own rites, rituals, modus operandi, and topics of conversation.

Companies can analyze the online culture established around their brand through the use of netnography, which will be detailed in Chapter 10. Corporations should be cognizant of the fact that through constant interactions, users may redefine Nike's brand and its values. The communication within the online community represents a means through which Nike can assess the extent to which the users' perceptions of corporate identity and values converge with those of the company. If there are drastic differences, it can be argued that users socially constructed Nike's brand through their interactions. Depending on the strength of the online network and its online influence, Nike may consider bringing additional connotations to its values or effectively communicating its values to reshape its followers' perceptions.

Because Nike addresses a community that has formed its own cyberculture, the company does not need to adapt its use of visuals and tailor them to a specific audience. It suffices to adapt the psychology of colors to its brand and values.

To conclude, this chapter discussed two strategies that companies can adopt to engage with their stakeholders abroad. The first, called the global approach, involves an adapting company values to build relationships differently in specific countries. The second way refers to creating an online community around an interest that is related to the brand. The latter strategy represents an international approach based on the premise that online users build their own cyberculture around a point of interest, which in turn renders their cultural differences irrelevant. Ideally, companies should consider the value of each approach and employ both international and global relationship management when appropriate to develop identification with a larger number of stakeholders.

CHAPTER 8

Corporate Activism

The present chapter tackles corporate activism, a fairly recent phenomenon through which corporations embrace social causes in an attempt to influence public policy and/or meet activist expectations. By looking at corporate efforts at Patagonia and IBM, the chapter delineates best practices in the United States and abroad and highlights advocacy aspects that could impede relationship management and corporate identification with consumers.

In 2023, the Axis Harris Poll ranked Patagonia as the most reputable brand in America (Axis Harris Poll 2023). Founded over 50 years ago by avid rock climber Yvon Chouinard, Patagonia's story dates back to his concern for the environment. Specifically, disappointed in the iron spikes used to secure ropes when climbing, Yvon Chouinard created his own version of pitons, which became known for their superior durability (Sundheim 2023). As climbing became popular and his business was booming, Chouinard witnessed the damage that pitons had on rocks during climbing. Despite the fact that pitons represented 70 percent of his business, Chouinard ceased their production and focused on the development of a new version of chocks, made of aluminum. Later, he successfully managed to dispel the climbers' general reticence toward chocks and to showcase their reliability by climbing the Nose route of El Captain (Sundheim 2023). By 1972, chock rock climbing had taken over the market and the use of pitons became negligible (Sundheim 2023). The popularity of aluminum chocks and their positive impact on the environment is attributed to Yvon Chouinard's spirit and vision, both of which laid the groundwork for Patagonia and continue to influence its mission. More precisely, Chouinard believed in communicating transparently about his products and innovating to diminish the negative impact on the environment. In sum, he put the environment ahead of profit.

Continuing his tradition, in 2007, Patagonia introduced the Footprint Chronicles, an initiative through which the company showcased the positive and the negative of each product it sold (Polley 2012). From a marketing perspective, the concept was terrifying, yet its positive reception signaled that consumers were not expecting perfection, but honesty. To date, the protagonist in Patagonia's story, Yvon Chouinard, along with his personal values, inspires the company's identity. Hence, Patagonia stands for integrity, quality, environmentalism, unconventionalism, and justice. The presence of these values is evident in the products developed with a focus on quality while keeping the environment in mind, products that are designed and developed by employees whose company avows to treat others fairly and equitably.

It can be argued that the ubiquitous presence of these values in the products triggers the customers' identification with Patagonia. For example, the consistent presence of quality and concern for the environment make the brand recognizable. When these values converge with those of the consumers, they encourage identification with the company and, in time, consumer loyalty. Undoubtedly, identification with Patagonia differs across the consumer base and is contingent upon the degree to which some of Patagonia's values carry more weight for consumers over other corporate values. Additionally, the concept of strategic ambiguity that the previous chapters discussed enables the identification of a large palette of consumers given that the values are broad enough to facilitate multiple interpretations.

One of the primary values that shape Patagonia's identity, namely environmentalism, is worth discussing in more detail, particularly when understanding corporate activism and what constitutes good practice. For some consumers, environmentalism is a primary concern and, therefore, they identify with Patagonia primarily through this value. By contrast, some consumers may value quality and unconventionalism to a greater degree than environmentalism. In the case of these consumers, their identification with the company and the relationship developed with Patagonia may in time produce a shift in perceptions to the point to which environmentalism becomes a primary concern. This shift emerges as a result of the parasocial relationship built with

Patagonia through the company's social media and marketing communication efforts. Therefore, by making environmentalism a concern for a multitude of consumers, Patagonia effectively engages in advocacy and raises awareness to engender positive change. It transforms regular consumers into concerned citizens who are likely to be more mindful of the environment as they go about their daily lives. By contrast, consumers for whom environmentalism is already a priority develop a relationship with a brand that is likely to strengthen their commitment to the cause.

One way that Patagonia promotes environmentalism beyond its products is through its partnerships with ambassadors who hail from countries that range from Australia to the United States and Chile. Renowned for their athletic achievements in climbing and surfing and also known for their environmental activism, the ambassadors' connection to the brand enables Patagonia to directly promote environmentalism and, indirectly, its products. The ambassadors are celebrated activists who cofounded their own advocacy organizations and/or testified before governments on environmental issues (Patagonia 2024). These ambassadors put a face to a successful brand and make it relatable to the general consumer. Further, relatability facilitates the establishment and fostering of a relationship with Patagonia. It is worth noting that brand ambassadors generally enjoy a large social media network that often represents a close-knit online community with recurrent online contributions and strong bonds among its members. By advocating for a brand, ambassadors "lend" their network to a corporation that can draw on the bonds between the ambassador and their online followers to foster corporate identification.

Patagonia is a case of successful corporate activism. Yet, recently, there have been several cases of corporate efforts that were met with backlash. These include Disney, Target, and Bud Light. Patagonia's success is a consequence of the organic emergence of environmental activism. In contrast to Disney, Target, and Bud Light, Patagonia's focus on environmentalism represented the very cornerstone of its foundation. Moreover, throughout its 50-year history, Patagonia has never ceased to advocate for the environment. For example, in 1985, Yvon Chouinard cofounded "One percent for the planet," an organization that unites corporations around the world in their effort to donate 1 percent of their profit to environmental causes.

As activist efforts have recently increased in American society, putting pressure on corporations to engage in what advocates referred to as "environmental justice," Patagonia did not have to make shift changes in its operations. The company had already been committed to environmental causes, which represented an essential aspect of its identity. By contrast, corporations that made abrupt changes and avowed to focus more on the environment were more likely to be viewed as disingenuous. In turn, perceptions of disingenuousness prevented such companies from establishing relationships with their potential consumers or in some cases, damaged existing ones, particularly as corporations backpaddled and left their consumers to wonder what their precise identity really was.

In this respect, a recent study that analyzed corporate activism in the wake of increased activism in the United States revealed that causes that do not align with a brand's values fail to exert a positive influence on a company's reputation (Lim and Young 2021). These results corroborate the findings of previous research on corporate social responsibility (CSR), which showed that CSR directly impacts corporate reputation as long as a company's CSR efforts aligned with its core values (Hydock, Neeru, and Weber 2019). Finally, research has shown that inconsistency in embracing causes, along with advocating for social issues in the aftermath of pressure from activists, has led to negative consumer perceptions and possible backlash (Maiorescu-Murphy 2022). Such negative perceptions emerge as stakeholders not only view the respective company as insincere, but they also grapple to understand its identity. This happens because the stance that the corporation takes today often differs from the stance it took a few years back.

As pressure from activist groups has mounted and American society has become more divided, corporations have found themselves in situations in which their very embracement of a societal cause equates with a political statement. For example, by taking a stance on environmental protection, a corporation might trigger perceptions of support for the Democratic party despite the fact that environmental concerns are universal. It is highly unlikely that currently, stakeholders view a corporation that embraces a societal issue as apolitical. The present societal divide in the United States, exacerbated by the media and politicians from both major political parties, corporations are well advised to embrace causes that directly relate to their values. By doing so, not only do they show sincere commitment but also diminish the likelihood that consumers will interpret advocacy as political.

What Is Corporate Activism?

The next paragraphs will delve into what precisely constitutes corporate advocacy and how it emerged as a concept in the business world.

In the 1970s, activists in the United States put corporations under the magnifying glass for their impact on the environment. The Committee for Economic Development, a nonprofit and nonpartisan public policy think tank, issued "social contracts" with one of the responsibilities being that corporations were to become involved in the macroenvironments in which they operated (Association of Corporate Citizenship Professionals 2024). This implied being cognizant of their impact on the environment and getting involved in communities. Consequently, the term CSR emerged in both theory and practice and much research was done to assess the impact of CSR on the bottom line. Studies from business and communication fields, sociology, anthropology, and psychology generally agreed that corporate contributions to society indirectly impact the bottom line by generating increased consumer loyalty and a more positive reputation, both of which serve as a buffer in times of corporate crises.

Corporations embraced CSR by developing and implementing community projects related to education, health, diversity and inclusion, and concern for the environment, to name a few. By the end of the 20th century, CSR was accepted as a prerequisite for business success. Today, the corporate responsibility index (CRI) assesses a company's societal impact through self-assessment surveys. High rankings represent the sine qua non to stay competitive on the market while anything less than that can severely tarnish corporate reputation. The delivery of quality products and services is seen as insufficient unless coupled with responsible citizenship.

By 2016, activism in the United States had increased in intensity, particularly with the rise of the Black Lives Matter Movement, which by that time had become a major global advocacy organization (Armitage 2016). A noticeable shift occurred at this time in corporate CSR, which became more intense and included communicative practices reminiscent of advocacy groups (Olkkonen and Jääskeläinen 2019). Illustrating the shift was Howard Schultz's 2015 "Race Together" campaign that encouraged Starbucks's patrons to discuss race and ethnicity (Lim and Young 2021). Through this campaign, Starbucks's CEO transcended the company's CSR value of diversity as equal treatment, equal opportunity, respect, and appreciation to push for global change. Researchers of the period coined the concept of "corporate responsibility to race" (CRR) to highlight the fact that corporations should be committed to improving race relations (Logan 2021). Further, the term corporate political advocacy (CPA), sometimes referred to as corporate activism, emerged in studies as researchers argued that corporations should genuinely advocate for causes without concern for financial consequences and consumer alienation (Ciszek and Logan 2018).

By contrast, some researchers contended that by advocating for societal causes that align with views espoused by political parties in the United States, corporations build a political identity that is likely to influence societal discourse and impact public policy (Atkinson 2017). Consequently, not all of a company's external stakeholders might perceive advocacy efforts as beneficial to society, irrespective of their views on certain causes. Negative perceptions may emerge, given that through the tremendous financial resources that corporations can invest in causes, they have the power to intrude on a domain reserved for governments that citizens elect by democratic vote. Moreover, activist groups that support a certain cause may influence corporate decision making, yet their opinions may not represent the entirety of views on a specific cause as espoused in their community. Therefore, corporations may influence public policy in ways that do not support the best interests of the majority or even an entire minority group.

By taking on a political identity, companies often deviate from a well-established identity that leads to the relationships they have previously developed. Consumers are left wondering what the company stands for, particularly when one of the causes that previously fell under the company's CSR umbrella has suddenly become its modus operandi. For example, if a company that previously committed to reducing its pollution as part of its CSR umbrella that also included health and educational programs, now abruptly decides to focus extensively on fighting climate change, its message may leave consumers confused. Additionally, the swift change might raise concerns about corporate intentions, particularly if it comes at a time when activism around the topic has intensified.

Several researchers have argued that corporations should genuinely focus on altruism and a sincere commitment to advocacy (Logan 2021). Yet, given the public's distrust of corporations and companies' swift shift from CSR to advocacy, it is doubtful that consumers will regard corporate activism as altruistic. As pointed out in Chapter 5, stakeholders are more likely to positively view a company that acknowledges the impact of embracing causes on its bottom line than one that communicates its true commitment to social causes. In other words, an honest stance could both win consumers and positively contribute to the environment. Above all, a corporate approach to societal causes that is effective and ethical cannot be undertaken without consulting the communities it affects. For this purpose, companies can make use of research to deeply engage the community they aim to assist. For example, social media communication, surveys, focus groups, and one-on-one interviews can be used to determine the most pressing issues that a community is facing and that a company can address. While activist groups pressure companies to embrace a certain cause, their efforts should serve as a catalyst for further discussions and for the understanding of the communities that activist groups aim to represent.

Corporate activism represents a new phenomenon whose long-term impact has yet to be assessed. By embracing causes intended to contribute to the well-being of the communities they serve, some corporations add to their positive reputation in the long run, while others may not recover from consumer backlash. The positive effects of corporate advocacy may be similar to those of CSR, provided that the causes that companies embrace do not deviate significantly from their already established identity.

Corporate Activism Abroad

Differences in the political and economic environments, activism, culture, and media systems make it harder for corporations to be consistent in their advocacy efforts on a global level. For example, in international environments, diversity may refer to socioeconomic status rather than ethnic, racial, and gender differences. This is particularly the case in countries low on immigration that tend to have a more homogenous population than the United States. Moreover, while the advancement of women in the workplace has been a focus in corporate America, Eastern cultures tend to value family over ascending the corporate ladder. In addition to cultural differences, low levels of activism, existing local legislation, dictatorial regimes, and the lack of free media impede corporate activism. Undoubtedly, communication professionals working for multinational corporations should conduct extensive local research before embarking on advocacy, particularly since the corporate values of one country may need to be adapted to other environments.

A practical approach to advocacy involves a broader appeal to a larger palette of stakeholders and adaptations for cultural differences. For example, Howard Schultz' 2015 "Race Together" enabled patrons across the world to define race according to their local experiences and their culture. More recently, IBM's 2024 Call for Code Global Challenge constitutes an initiative aimed at a global collaboration among students and software developers from academia and industry to build AI solutions for issues such as climate change, clean water, and safe and affordable housing (IBM 2024). Through this initiative, IBM advocates for solutions to social issues while aligning the project with its business profile (tech) and values (CSR). Therefore, this advocacy effort does not deviate from the company's identity, particularly as IBM had engaged in similar initiatives before. What has changed are the specific causes that the company is advocating for, such as climate change, a cause aligned with current activism in the United States. Above all, this challenge enables collaborators to discuss safe housing, clean water, and climate change from their own perspectives and in accord with their own culture. Therefore, it can be argued that IBM takes a bottom-up approach and gives voice to those who know how the issues affect them the most. By contrast, IBM could have conducted research in specific countries and engaged in activism based on the company's findings. However, by taking a bottom-up approach, the company has demonstrated genuine commitment to the issues, thus strengthening its relationships with existing consumers and likely encouraging corporate identification with its worldwide collaborators. The positive ramifications of this project are therefore global as the company shows commitment and its efforts align with its identity.

This chapter discussed the impact of corporate activism on relationships with external stakeholders (consumers) and the degree to which they identify with a company. Corporate activism is still a relatively new phenomenon. Consumers may meet it with boycotts or "buycotts" depending on the degree to which advocacy falls under their system of beliefs as well as the extent to which they regard advocacy efforts as genuine and part of a company's already established identity.

CHAPTER 9

Crisis and Scandal Management

The present chapter discusses external crisis and scandal management by looking at negative events that emerged at Toyota and Christian Dior. These illustrations provide an opportunity to introduce crisis and scandal management and to discuss possible ways to diminish the negative impact of crises and scandals on consumer relationships and corporate reputation.

From Johnson & Johnson's 1982 Tylenol crisis to the 2010 Deepwater Horizon oil spill, and, more recently, the FAA's 2024 investigation into Boeing's 737 Max, crises have rocked the corporate world and led researchers to study similarities among them and propose ways to avert or address them. Similar crises have emerged across industries and at different moments in time, a fact that showcases that it is oftentimes impossible to shun a crisis. Above all, many companies emerged renewed and stronger after a crisis, learning lessons that improved their products, services, and operations. In fact, in Greek, the very word "crisis" connotes both a negative event and an opportunity. There could perhaps be no better example than General Motors, whose renewal in the aftermath of the 2014 ignition switch recall was discussed in previous chapters. To manage a crisis effectively, companies have to focus on not losing consumer trust. Similar to the interpersonal relationships that we foster and that survive negative events as long as we do not lose trust in our partners, corporate relationships withstand turmoil if companies manage to deter the erosion of consumer trust. To maintain trust, corporations have to demonstrate that a crisis is an outlier rather than a modus operandi, and they must communicate their willingness to alter operations to prevent similar events from reoccurring.

Crisis Management

In January 2024, Toyota's Chairman, Akio Toyoda, expressed remorse for the company's recent safety crises. He contended:

> I would like to express my deepest apologies to our customers and stakeholders for the inconvenience and concern caused by the successive irregularities at Hino Motors, Daihatsu and Toyota Industries. (Pandolfo, 2024)

Mr. Toyoda's apology came in the aftermath of an external investigation that included 64 vehicle models and revealed data fabrication and safety test tampering (Pandolfo 2024). As a result of this investigation, the company suspended the shipment of the car models in question (Pandolfo 2024). This investigation occurred one month after Daihatsu, one of Toyota's subsidiaries, had put its production line on hold over similar concerns. Finally, in 2022, Hino Motors, another Toyota subsidiary, became embroiled in an emissions scandal (Pandolfo 2024).

Toyota's response to the preceding crises can be considered effective for two reasons. First, the company took corrective action by suspending the shipment of car models with questionable safety test results and evidence of data fabrication. By taking these measures, the company showcased that it prioritized its customers' safety and focused on implementing measures to prevent similar crises from recurring. Such measures reassured consumers that Toyota remained a trustworthy brand. The Chairman's apology appealed to the consumers' emotional needs and denoted respect by acknowledging wrongdoing. More often than not, consumers demonstrate that they continue to trust corporations despite their transgressions so long as the companies take corrective action and express remorse. For example, as of April 2024, Toyota has remained the best-selling car manufacturer worldwide (Pandolfo 2024).

Corrective action and apology represent effective crisis management strategies that have been empirically tested in research for decades. These strategies derive from the development of the situational crisis communication theory (SCCT) (Coombs 2020, 2022; Coombs and Tachkova 2024) that has been extensively studied and applied to practice (Figure 9.1).

According to the SCCT, when a company face a crisis, they first have to determine the situation they find themselves in or the type of crisis that they face. Crises can be classified as: (1) accidents (crises that could not have been prevented), (2) preventable crises, and (3) situations in which the company itself is a victim of the crisis. Determining the type of crisis that a company faces is essential, given that consumers will attribute a degree of responsibility to the company that is commensurate with the type of crisis that the corporation faces. For example, a corporation will be held accountable to a larger extent if its crisis classifies as preventable rather than an accident. By contrast, when the company itself is the victim of a crisis, stakeholders may attribute no responsibility to the organization. Compare Toyota's recent situation to Johnson & Johnson's 1982 Tylenol crisis whose culprit has not yet been found. Several Tylenol bottles had been laced with potassium cyanide, leading to deaths that Johnson & Johnson could not have prevented. By contrast, Toyota's recent and successive crises are classified as preventable as its subsidiaries could have averted data fabrication.

Strategy	Explanation	Example
Denial	1. Attack the accuser 2. Deny the crisis 3. Shift the blame	1. "The media coverage was dishonest." 2. "This never happened." 3. "The competition created a false narrative. "
Diminish the crisis	1. Minimize responsibility 2. Justify the negative event	1. "Top management had never been made aware of this situation." 2. "It happened because the company had to avoid bankruptcy."
Restore trust/Prevent loss of trust	1. Corrective action 2. Apology	1. "We have created a program of accountability that will ensure the safety of our vehicles." 2. "We are sorry."
Bolstering	Discuss the past positive impact on communities	"We have always been dedicated to our communities. For example, our educational programs have so far helped over 2,000 children in the area."

Figure 9.1 The situational crisis communication theory, (Coombs 2020)

Because consumers likely attributed a high degree of responsibility to Toyota, the company took corrective action and apologized.

According to the SCCT, determining the type of crisis enables companies to take an appropriate approach without underreacting or overacting to a negative event, both of which could lead to decreased consumer trust. For example, a multinational company that faces an unavoidable accident in the United States is not likely to be held accountable by its consumers given that the crisis could not have been prevented. While the company should address the crisis and discuss it in the media, it is recommended that it does not engage in extensive crisis communication abroad. Should the company employ substantial communication practices in countries in which the accident has no repercussions, it might draw additional attention to a negative event that has no implications abroad. Doing so can actually damage consumer relationships and seed skepticism toward the brand.

Thus far we have seen that the crisis type can lead consumers to attribute a significant or less significant degree of responsibility to a company. However, corporate reputation and no history of crises influence the extent to which consumers attribute responsibility to the company that currently faces crises. According to the SCCT, a positive corporate reputation and no history of crises represent significant buffers that can protect corporate reputation and prevent the erosion of consumer trust (Coombs 2020). Specifically, Toyota had enjoyed a strong reputation before the recent data fabrication crisis. In turn, the reputation enabled the company to maintain consumer trust. As for a history of crises, it is worth mentioning that Toyota experienced a major negative event in 2010 as the company issued recalls for a faulty accelerator that had resulted in a significant number of victims. At that time, the company took delayed corrective action. It responded by shifting the bulk of the blame to government agencies, including the National Highway Traffic Safety Administration (NHTSA), and provided explanations, seen by many as excuses, for its delayed recalls (Maiorescu 2016). Consequently, at that time, consumers attributed a high degree of responsibility to the company. Yet, the company managed to restore consumer trust in the following 14 years through consistent delivery of quality and safe vehicles and therefore enjoyed a strong corporate reputation at the time of its most recent crises.

Corporate reputation is an extremely relevant element in determining consumer trust, consumer identification with a company, and corporate-consumer relationships. Corporate reputation represents the totality of consumer perceptions of a company over an extended period of time. It emerges as a result of quality products and services, the company's involvement in the community, sustainability, purchase experiences, as well as the actual experiences that consumers have with a product or service. A positive corporate reputation forms the basis of consumer trust. Consumers identify with companies that enjoy positive reputations and whose avowed values converge with their own. A negative reputation implies serious corporate transgressions or low-quality products and services, all of which would contradict the very values that a corporation has promoted.

To manage a crisis, the SCCT identified several communication strategies that should be carefully employed, depending on the type of crisis. These response strategies include denial which emerges when a company (1) attacks the accuser, (2) denies the crisis, and (3) shifts blame. These strategies should be reserved for cases when the company itself is a victim of the crisis, as in the Tylenol crisis. It is worth noting that such crises occur extremely rarely. Additional primary strategies include those that aim to diminish a crisis and can involve communication practices that attempt to (1) minimize the responsibility of a company for a crisis and (2) justify the negative event. Companies may consider employing diminishing strategies in case of accidents and crises that they could not have prevented. For example, if an employee gets injured at their workplace and the company has taken all the safety measures possible to avoid it, corporate representatives can provide justifications for the unfortunate event. By providing such explanations, representatives deliver clarity and persuasion. Finally, rebuilding strategies are meant to restore consumer trust or avert its erosion in the case of preventable crises. These strategies include (1) taking corrective action and (2) issuing an apology, as illustrated in Toyota's data fabrication example. By taking corrective action, companies ensure that there are no additional victims of the crisis. Hence, corrective action addresses consumers' physical needs, while the purpose of an apology is to appeal to their emotional ones (Coombs 2020). Oftentimes, companies cannot immediately appeal to the emotional needs of their consumers due to litigation concerns and ongoing external investigations, which usually impede the issuance of an apology.

The preceding strategies are considered primary responses based on past research studies that employed the SCCT and that revealed their effectiveness in averting the loss of consumer trust or restoring it. Further, bolstering strategies represent secondary crisis communication that companies may consider in addition to their primary response. Bolstering refers to communicative acts through which companies remind their consumers of their positive past deeds (Coombs 2020). In other words, corporations refer to their positive corporate reputation or contributions to their communities in an attempt to signal that the present crisis does not reflect their identity and values.

In conclusion, companies can effectively apply the SCCT to the type of crisis they face. Communication professionals should regularly monitor and scan consumer perceptions during a crisis. As the media continues to cover a crisis and as online users communicate about it, consumer perceptions may fluctuate or change. For example, a company may experience a crisis that is classified as an accident. It can be easily argued that the company could not have prevented it and that it had little to no control over it. However, social media communication may indicate that users may view it as a preventable crisis for which they hold the company accountable. Hence, responding to this crisis by employing strategies that are effective in case of accidents may actually tarnish the corporate reputation. Additionally, a media coverage analysis may indicate the presence of a slant, which could lead the general public to view the crisis as preventable. Companies have to adapt their crisis response strategies to changing perceptions. In the end, it doesn't matter if a corporation is responsible for a crisis or not if its consumers believe that it is. Hence, the company has to provide the response necessary to convince them to the contrary (Coombs 2020).

Scandal Management

Whether preventable or not, the crises that corporations face are generally revealed to the public by the media. Oftentimes, corporations themselves inform the public about a crisis, and by doing so, they more effectively avert the negative impact of the event on their relationship with consumers. By defining the crisis first, companies showcase their commitment to ensuring safety. They prove that they are worthy of trust as they proactively take measures meant to avert the future reoccurrence of similar crises. By contrast, if the media defines a corporate crisis first, any measure that a company takes is viewed as reactive and defensive, possibly leading to the erosion of consumer trust. Finally, when an external entity, such as the media, is the first to communicate about the crisis, the company may lose control over it because the negative event is framed in ways beyond the corporation's control.

However, there are crises that are neither defined by the media nor by companies, but rather by social media users. Researchers refer to these crises as scandals and argue that, unlike negative events, such as accidents and preventable crises, scandals emerge as social media users express moral outrage toward a corporation for products, services, or business operations (Coombs and Tachkova 2019, 2024). Christian Dior's Sauvage scandal represents an illustration of how quickly moral outrage can spread online to force a corporation to take action. In 2019, Dior released a new ad for its perfume, Sauvage, featuring Native American actor, Johnny Depp. The ad, shot in Utah, included Native American dances and ended with Johnny Depp's statement "We are the land. The new Sauvage—le parfum Dior" (Maiorescu-Murphy 2021). Within 24 hours, the social media backlash was significant enough to force the company to withdraw the ad (Means 2019). Online users expressed moral outrage as they perceived the advertisement as a form of cultural appropriation and insensitivity, particularly given the connotation of the word Sauvage, which translates into English as "savage" (Maiorescu-Murphy 2021). In addition to taking corrective action by withdrawing the ad, the company responded and emphasized its respect for the Native American culture. For example, Dior representatives indicated that they had collaborated with the Americans for Indian

Opportunity (AIO), a nonprofit organization with a long tradition of advocating for the promotion of the Native American culture and rights (Perez 2019), and discussed the collaboration with Johnny Depp, a member of the Comanche Nation (Maiorescu-Murphy 2021; Means 2019). However, Dior's detailed response failed to put an end to the negative reactions on social media. Consequently, the company withdrew its campaign.

The moral outrage to Dior's campaign that was present online, particularly on X, did not emerge in a vacuum but rather in a context of increased activism in the American society that called for closer scrutiny of corporations in general and into the luxury fashion industry in particular. While the fashion industry had always drawn on cultures for the purpose of creativity in design (Pozzo 2020) and marketing communications (Maiorescu-Murphy 2021), it had been placed under the magnifying glass for making a profit off of motifs, traditions, and folklore, which had never been protected by copyrights legislation. In other words, activist groups and the general public had started to view cultural appropriation as a breach of morality: companies profit while making use of the culture of some particular group who, in turn, receives no remuneration. Moreover, cultural appropriation began to be viewed as a breach of morality given that corporations, as outsiders to a specific culture, were perceived to define it, pack it, and commercialize it, therefore, deviating from the traditions specific to an ethnic group (Greaves 1994; Maiorescu-Murphy 2021). Specifically, corporations began to be seen as the modifiers of the cultures they were drawing on.

Today, research on scandal management is still in its early stages. It emerged to study consumer perceptions in response to various issues as they related to the increased activism that has occurred in recent years. Thus far, research has shown that, while in the case of regular crises, the public exhibits anger, when it comes to scandals, stakeholders display moral outrage, a much deeper form of emotion (Coombs and Tachkova 2019; Grebe 2012, Maiorescu-Murphy 2021). Furthermore, corporations can address anger and appease consumers in the aftermath of a crisis through corrective action and apology. By contrast, because moral outrage represents a stronger emotion, the public is likely to take revenge by punishing the corporation they hold accountable for transgressions (Coombs and Tachkova 2019, 2024; Maiorescu-Murphy 2021). The punishment can range from boycotts to significant negative communication on social media, all of which may tarnish reputation, lead to decreased trust, erode consumer identification, and damage consumer relationships. Because the public or subsets of it may likely seek revenge, it is possible that the crisis responses recommended via the SCCT may not be applicable or that they should be refined to address moral outrage (Coombs and Tachkova 2019, 2024). For example, despite the fact that Dior's response included vast explanations about the advertisement campaign, negative online communication ceased only after the company withdrew its ad. It is also worth mentioning that Dior had been using the name of its perfume Sauvage since 1966. While it can be argued that the company displayed a lack of cultural sensitivity in its ad, it can equally be asserted that at least some online users displayed unwillingness to listen to Dior's response.

The scarce research that exists on scandal management (Antonetti and Maklan 2016; Coombs and Tachkova 2019, 2024; Maiorescu-Murphy 2021) highlights certain factors that communication professionals can take into account as they determine whether a scandal may tarnish the corporate reputation and consumer relationship. First, the *severity* of the scandal is of utmost importance. Professionals can analyze user-generated communication to ascertain how severe online users perceive the transgression to be. Second, companies have to assess how much of the user-generated communication reveals that users perceive that the company had *control* over the scandal and did not prevent it. Third, an additional aspect to consider represents the extent to which the users' communication denotes that the company committed an *injustice*. In other words, when it comes to the perceived transgression, did the corporation bring about injustice toward a group or an individual? Fourth, moral outrage is exacerbated by the extent to which online users regard the perceived transgression as motivated by *greed*, which in turn led the company to exploit a group/individual (Coombs and Tachkova 2019, 2024). For the purpose of this assessment, communication professionals can make use of thematic analyses, whose application is discussed in Chapter 10.

As a scandal unfolds, it is paramount that companies conduct necessary assessments regularly, possibly daily. While this analysis requires a significant investment of time, its results can reveal shifts in perceptions and therefore enable an appropriate response without overacting or underreacting to the scandal. Because scandals emerge on social media through communication practices among users, they continue to be defined and redefined via their interactions. Undoubtedly, the extent to which scandals flourish online is contingent upon the strength of the users' online network as determined by the number of followers and the extent to which they make recurrent online contributions.

In the case of Dior's scandal, an analysis on X that applied the preceding factors over a period of 12 months from the day the scandal emerged determined that the majority of social communication revolved around perceived injustice, greed, and controllability. To a lesser degree, users defined injustice as double societal standards vis-à-vis the folklore pertaining to other ethnic groups, such as the Irish American community and the general population's celebration of Saint Patrick's Day, which was not viewed as cultural appropriation (Maiorescu-Murphy 2021). These deep emotions that dominated social media communication render Dior's ad withdrawal justified. By doing so after providing explanations about the ad, the company preserved consumer trust and maintained the already established consumer relationships. It demonstrated that, while unwittingly committing an act that was perceived as a breach of morality, it was malleable enough to immediately respond to stakeholder expectations.

Companies invest significant time, effort, and resources in averting crises and scandals. However, oftentimes, these cannot be prevented despite numerous crisis management plans that generally include detailed information about possible future events. Avoiding scandals altogether may prove an even more arduous task, given the multitude of divergent perceptions that surface on social media platforms. In addition, social media sites are built and structured around giving voice to consumers. Their voice can improve corporate products, services, operations, and community engagement. The more robust a relationship between a company and its consumers and the stronger the identification between the two, the more likely consumers are to provide feedback that can improve corporate functions. Yet, online users may also display moral outrage that can significantly impact corporate reputation unless addressed promptly. For this purpose, communication professionals should constantly engage in issues scanning to determine negative online communication that has the potential to develop into a crisis or a scandal. Daily scanning of the social media environment should consist not only of the issues that surface online but should also entail a rank order based on the probability that each issue will develop into a crisis/scandal and its potential severity. To rank order the issues, practitioners should consider the following: (1) The environmental variables, including the political environment, economy, culture, level of activism, and the media. In countries high on activism that enjoy a free media system, issues are likely to quickly go viral and set the media's agenda. In turn, media coverage will generate more social media communication as users share news articles. (2) The influence that the users have online, which can be determined by conducting a network analysis. Software available for this purpose, such as NodeXL, UCInet, and Gephi, can reveal the number of users that participate in a specific online discussion and the extent to which they have a strong online influence.

This chapter looked at crisis and scandal management and highlighted the difference between the two. While crises can be addressed via the application of the SCCT, there is little that we know about effective responses to scandals. Thus far, scandals seem to emerge in the backdrop of intense activism and social movements. Therefore, it is important for companies to develop and promote their products in line with their community engagement programs. For example, if a company provides scholarships to disadvantaged children, its marketing communication practices should reflect empathy toward its consumers and the community. This ensures the consistent implementation of corporate values, a consistency needed to build and maintain relationships with consumers.

Finally, to complicate matters more, a crisis can lead to a scandal (Coombs and Tachkova 2019). For example, if a company does not issue a timely recall of a contaminated product and the media reveals that it purposefully hid information from the public, its decision to not take action can cause moral outrage. Consumers are likely to feel betrayed and justifiably so, as they view that the company put profit ahead of their well-being. Undoubtedly, they will lose trust in the brand and withdraw from the relationship established with the company. To prevent a crisis from developing into a scandal, companies should manage it by applying the SCCT to prove that their consumers come first. Additionally, communication professionals should constantly monitor social media platforms and reactions to the company's crisis response to ascertain the presence of the various scandal factors.

CHAPTER 10

Assessing Relationship Management

This book has detailed the development and management of relationships with stakeholder groups, in general, and with primary stakeholder groups, including employees and consumers, in particular. The previous chapters have discussed the role that corporate values and corporate identity play in relationship management in both internal and external corporate settings. For example, internally, we have examined the role played by leadership styles, employee engagement techniques, and diversity and inclusion. Externally, we have discussed global and local approaches that companies can adopt to foster relationships with consumers, the role of corporate activism in shaping corporate identification, as well as ways to address scandals and crises in order to avoid damaging consumer relationships. The present chapter investigates how companies can make use of research, particularly as it relates to user-generated communication that builds and maintains relationships. To this end, the chapter will focus on research methodologies that are not widely used in the corporate world, including ethnography, netnography, and autoethnography. These methods can provide invaluable insight into corporate identification and relationship management.

The corporate world is making extensive use of quantitative research methods, including surveys, sentiment analyses, and network analyses. By contrast, the methodologies discussed next pertain to the domain of qualitative, interpretative, and subjective research that represent essential tools for building relationships around corporate values that foster corporate identification. Before we delve into the specifics of each methodology, it is important to note that they require minimum financial investment and, therefore, represent an accessible way to understand how to effectively build relationships. For example, analyzing internal social media platforms and observing the employee culture in the workplace may reveal significant insights that can inform relationship-building strategies without the use of more costly research methods such as surveys, interviews, and focus groups. At the very least, qualitative methods can provide important clarifications with respect to employee and consumer expectations and can refine questions that should be further investigated through surveys, interviews, and focus groups.

Ethnography

In the corporate world, building relationships with employees and consumers is a task frequently relegated to the communication department. The task can be daunting, whether it involves building relationships on internal social media platforms or offline through event planning, newsletters, and trainings. In general, practitioners determine the effectiveness of their social media strategy by assessing the interactivity it generates. Interactivity is measured in likes, reposts, new followers, and so on, and practitioners monitor on a regular basis. Undoubtedly, interactivity is extremely important. Yet, communication practices that emerge in the users' interactions are equally relevant. In the workplace, corporations often send out yearly surveys to assess the internal culture and to find ways to build relationships across the employee base. Yet, regular observations of the employee culture are also important.

For the purpose of clarity with respect to research methods, let's consider a hypothetical example. Imagine that you spend six months abroad for business purposes. Let's assume that you travel to Montego Bay where you rent an apartment. As you get to know your neighbors, walk around the streets, interact with the locals, try different restaurants, and so on, you start to develop an understanding of Jamaican culture. You get to be exposed to some of the Jamaican rites, rituals, preferences, and communication styles. For example, you notice that in Montego Bay people are less in a hurry and more prone to interact with strangers than in the United States. They also love to show you around and they take immense pride in the picturesque landscape of their island. Their communication style is other-centered as they try to make you feel welcome and to ensure that you have what you need for an enjoyable stay. Your observations constitute what anthropologists refer to as an ethnography or an ethnographic study. If you record your observations in a notebook, these will represent your field notes. If both you and I went to Montego Bay, our field notes may slightly differ because, ultimately, ethnography is subjective. We each see a phenomenon and interpret a culture through a unique lens. Yet, both of us are likely to agree on major aspects that we noticed, such as hospitality and friendliness.

From a corporate perspective, ethnography helps us to understand the culture of our consumers and employees. For example, our preceding ethnography example could inform Citibank's marketing campaigns in Jamaica. Similarly, a communication practitioner working for Starbucks in the United States can regularly visit Starbucks coffee shops and observe the interactions among the consumers, take note of their topics of conversation, their communication style, and so on. These observations, too, constitute an ethnographic study. The implications can inform how Starbucks promotes its values and develops relationships around them. The results of the ethnographic study would enable the company to communicate on social media platforms by emulating the culture of the consumers as observed in its stores. This implies tackling topics of consumer interest, embedding visuals that depict the consumers' style, and emulating their communication practices. An ethnographic study can additionally inform offline relationship management, ranging from event planning and community engagement to advertising campaigns. By shedding light on the culture of the consumers, ethnographic insights enable companies to better relate their values to consumer expectations and, therefore, facilitate corporate identification.

Internally, communication professionals are immersed in the workplace culture and, therefore, it can be argued that they conduct ethnographies on a daily basis. Their insights can inform the communication practices to be used on internal social media platforms to strengthen identification with the company and its values. The previous chapters discussed the concept of online communities and the importance of building relationships and fostering corporate identification. When practitioners aim to build an online community on internal social media platforms, the insights they gain through their daily ethnographies allow them to emulate online the employee culture they observe at the office. By doing so, they increase the likelihood that the employees will not only join the online platform but they will also contribute regular content.

In conclusion, the culture of the internal social media platform should mirror the offline culture of the group it aims to attract and keep. This same principle applies to external social media communication. Ethnographic insights enable practitioners to create content that emulates the offline culture of their employees or consumers. In sum, ethnography provides a deep understanding of a culture and reveals rites, rituals, beliefs, motivations, preferences, and communication styles that effectively inform relationship building and maintenance (Brewer 2000).

Netnography

Let's assume you have already built an online community for either your employees or your consumers. As discussed in the previous chapters, you notice recurrent contributions from regular users who display familiarity with one another and with past topics discussed in the online group. It is evident that your communication strategy yielded results and that you have indeed built an online community. These recurrent contributions have led to the establishment of a cyberculture that is specific to this community. The online interactions lead in time to group rites, rituals, and ways of communication that are unique. Hence, you can make use of the user-generated data to conduct an ethnography. Because the analysis is conducted online, the literature refers to this methodology as "netnography" (Kozinets 2015). A netnography is less intrusive because, unless you let the online users know that you study their communication, your analysis does not intrude on the group's culture. As long as the data are public (in the case of the external social media platforms) or are available internally to the entire employee base (in the case of internal social media platforms), practitioners should not consider their decisions unethical. However, if they do wish to reveal to the online community that they conduct a netnography, they should be aware that from that moment on, it is likely that online interactions will decrease or that they will not be as genuine as in the past. Thus, by conducting research, practitioners slightly change the group's culture.

It is important to note that the same principle of disclosed research applies to conducting ethnographies. Practitioners may or may not disclose that they observe an offline culture. Should they disclose this, they should anticipate that interactions may change and that they may never get to experience completely the culture in its real form. Consider the previous example about Montego Bay. If you told the locals that you are studying their customs, rites, and communication styles, do you think they would be their regular selves? It is likely that they would become more reserved or distant than usual; therefore, your analysis may be limited.

However, in the case of both ethnography and netnography, when practitioners disclose that they conduct research, they gain the opportunity to ask questions that they wouldn't otherwise, particularly when it comes to technical ones related to consumer expectations or corporate identification. Such questions would be perceived as out of place in everyday conversations that occur when practitioners choose not to disclose that they conduct research. Hence, it behooves the practitioners to determine the best course of action, which should be a decision based on the specific purpose of the netnography/ethnography they conduct and the type of answers that they are expecting.

The greatest advantage of netnography represents the fact that it is a nonintrusive method. In the case of an ethnography conducted in a coffee shop with regular consumers, a stranger's presence may slightly modify the interactions and communication practices of a close-knit group. After all, the practitioner is an intruder into a space frequented by regular consumers. Therefore, in the case of an online community, unless practitioners inform its members of their intention to conduct an analysis, a netnography would equate with "lurking." Yet, the greatest disadvantage of netnographies over ethnographies lies in their lack of nonverbal communication. User-generated content lacks verbal cues and body language, which comprises most of the overall communication process that would allow for a deep understanding of a specific culture.

Irrespective of visuals such as photos or videos, users may include written posts; these are controlled, edited, and cannot render real-time reactions.

Autoethnography

There may be perhaps no better start toward the understanding of corporate identification than by taking an introspective approach. If practitioners pause and think about their own experiences as employees and consumers, their insights can inform and shape further relationship management research that they aim to conduct. The methodology is called autoethnography and has been fairly recently applied to business studies (Lloyd-Parkes 2021). It was first introduced by award-winning anthropologist Ruth Behar in 1997 in the monograph entitled *The Vulnerable Observer: Anthropology That Breaks Your Heart.* The book details her journey to America as a Jewish Cuban immigrant by using a combination of ethnography and memoir. However, Behar acknowledges the challenges of revealing personal details while employing this methodology (Behar 2022).

Let's assume that an internal communication manager who works for Google aims to understand how employees identify with the company's value of building belonging at work, through products, and in society. An autoethnography would take the shape of a journal in which the manager would take daily notes of what belonging at the workplace has felt like for them personally. The manager would also have to view himself or herself as a consumer and jot down how it feels to experience Google's various products. Finally, the manager will consider that he or she is solely a citizen who does not have any employment relationship with Google, in which case the manager will take daily notes of how they see the company's contributions to society.

Autoethnography is highly subjective, yet can serve as grounds for further research. In the preceding hypothetical case, the manager could use the insights from his or her journal to create questions for an employee survey that would shed further light on what belonging in the workplace means across the employee base.

So far, the chapter has discussed three qualitative methodologies: ethnography, netnography, and autoethnography, all of which require the consistent recording of observations. The next step is for the practitioner to re-read these observations multiple times and refine them, adding more thoughts and observations, if needed. This process requires several exposures to the text. Then, the practitioner should employ what is referred to as a "thematic analysis." The analysis involves additional exposures to the final observations to determine recurrent themes that emerge in the text (Braun and Clarke 2006; Maguire and Delahunt 2017). Namely, are there any repetitive observations that could form a cluster? The exposure should continue until no new themes surface. Each theme should be titled. In the hypothetical example concerning Google's value of belonging, the internal communication manager may find a recurrent theme that they entitle "jovial conversations in the cafeteria." It is imperative that practitioners keep the data organized and that, once they've determined the main themes and have titled them, they next place each observation under its appropriate title.

This process of categorizing is particularly important given that, after they have ascertained the main themes, practitioners have to expose themselves to the text once again and determine the emergence of subthemes, if any (Braun and Clarke 2006; Maguire and Delahunt 2017). More precisely, they will have to analyze whether any recurrent observations emerge under each theme. For example, the analysis at Google may reveal recurrent observations about jovial conversations on raising children. Therefore, this represents a subtheme that could be labeled "raising children." Establishing subthemes is paramount because it provides an even deeper insight into what may make Google employees feel that they belong. Now the company has information that can be used to create family-centered events and can generate internal social media communication around the topic of raising children. A thematic analysis concludes when no additional themes and subthemes emerge in the text (Braun and Clarke 2006; Maguire and Delahunt 2017). Several programs such as NVivo provide for good organization of the data. However, unlike quantitative data generated through surveys, sentiment analyses, and network analyses, the software available for thematic analyses does not perform the analyses per se. Rather, they provide more reliability for the results given that they allow for good organization.

The three methods discussed in this chapter, while subjective, represent important steps toward determining how to form relationships and how to adapt corporate communication to improve them. They can be used to build relationships among employees, between leadership and employees, and between a company and its consumers both in offline and online settings. Relationships are rooted in dialogue and communication. As individuals, if we stop communicating, our relationships come to an end. The richness of the communication process cannot be ascertained solely by scales provided in surveys or by determining the most influential users in our online community via network analysis. While the importance of the preceding methods cannot be denied, the richness of human interactions should also be assessed through the lens of culture by using ethnographies, netnographies, and autoethnographies. Above all, the results of these analyses can address a myriad of questions that practitioners may have wanted to ask through surveys or, at the very least, shape these questions for a more focused and strategic survey methodology. This, in turn, saves a company resources, including time and money.

To conclude, this book provided a journey into relationship management. It argued that similar to the way individuals connect around the perceived similarity of values, so do corporations and their stakeholders. Through the convergence of values, stakeholders identify with a company and become more loyal employees or consumers. Contrary to everyday relationships, there is a tremendous power imbalance between the two entities when company relationships are involved. However, if corporations foster transparent communication and trust, all parties can benefit: employees have a workplace where they feel appreciated and where opportunities abound, consumers benefit from products and services of higher quality, and finally, corporations make an increased profit.

References

Abbas, T. "Kodak Change Management Failure." *Change Management Insight.* March 4, 2023. http://tinyurl.com/bn76musn.

Ahn, S.B. 2021. "An Essay About the Concept of 'Story Value': Necessity of Homo Narraticus and Enjoyment of Homo Narrans." *The Journal of Culture Contents 22*: 35–65.

Aichner, T., M. Grünfelder, O. Matthias, and D. Jegeni. 2021. "Twenty-Five Years of Social Media: A Review of Social Media Applications and Definitions from 1994 to 2019." *Cyberpsychology, behavior, and social networking 24*(4): 215–222.

Antonetti, P and S. Maklan. 2016 "An Extended Model of Moral Outrage at Corporate Social Irresponsibility." *Journal of Business Ethics* 135. 429–444.

Applebaum, L., F. Walton and K. Southerland. 2015. "An Examination of Factors Affecting Success of Underrepresented Groups in the Public Relations Profession," *Public Relations Society of America Foundation,*1–55. https://bit.ly/2w8z7jt.

Armitage, S. 2016. "2016 Was the Year Black Lives Matter Went Global." Buzzfeed News, December 8, 2016. https://tinyurl.com/3kjsu4zd. Accessed April 13, 2024.

Association of Corporate Citizenship Professionals. "Updated: Corporate Social Responsibility: A Brief History." https://tinyurl.com/4pvbfbmt (Accessed April 13, 2024).

Atkinson, J.D. 2017. *Journey into Social Activism: Qualitative Approaches.* Fordham University Press.

Axis Harris Poll. May 23, 2023. "The 2023 Axios Harris Poll 100 Reputation Rankings." Accessed April 12, 2024. https://tinyurl.com/2c4svhyk.

Bakker, A.B., J. Hetland, K.O. Olav and E. Roar. 2023. "Daily Transformational Leadership: A Source of Inspiration for Follower Performance?" *European Management Journal 41*(5): 700–708.

Barrabi, T. March 24, 2022 "Conservative Disney Employees Urge Company to Stay 'Politically Neutral.'" *The New York Post.* Accessed January 12, 2024 http://tinyurl.com/bdju975n.

Bass, B.M and R.E. Riggio. 2010 "The Transformational Model of Leadership." *Leading organizations: Perspectives for a New Era 2*(1): 76–86.

Bassett-Jones, N., 2005 "The Paradox of Diversity Management, Creativity and Innovation." *Creativity and innovation management* 14(2): 169–175.

Basu, T. "Timeline: A History of GM's Ignition Switch Defect." *NPR.* March 31, 2014. Accessed September 30, 2023. https://tinyurl.com/3a8zndep.

Behar, R. 2022. *The Vulnerable Observer: Anthropology that Breaks your Heart.* Beacon Press.

Behrooz, M., S. Reid and J. Arnav. 2015. "Remember that Time? Telling Interesting stories from Past Interactions." In *Interactive Storytelling: 8th International Conference on Interactive Digital Storytelling, ICIDS 2015,* 93–104 *Copenhagen, Denmark, November 30–December 4, 2015, Proceedings 8.* Springer International Publishing.

Braun, V and V. Clarke, V. 2006 "Using Thematic Analysis in Psychology." *Qualitative research in psychology* 3(2): 77–101.

Brewer, John. *Ethnography.* McGraw-Hill Education (UK), 2000.

Buntz, B. July 31, 2023. "Timeline: Navigating Johnson & Johnson's Talc Lawsuits and their Stock performance Impact." *Pharmaceutical Processing World.* Accessed January 8, 2024. http://tinyurl.com/532c6khn.

Burke, P.J and E.S. Jan. 2022. *Identity Theory: Revised and Expanded.* Oxford University Press.

Ciszek, E and N. Logan. 2018. "Challenging the Dialogic Promise: How Ben & Jerry's Support for Black Lives Matter fosters Dissensus on Social Media." *Journal of Public Relations Research* 30(3): 115–127.

Compton, J., W. Shelley and A.S. Sergei. 2021. "Inoculation Theory and Public Relations." *Public Relations Review* 47(5): 102116.

Coombs, W. T. 2020. "Situational Crisis Communication Theory: Influences, Provenance, Evolution, and Prospects." *Crisis Communication* : 121–140.

Coombs, W. T. "Situational Crisis Communication Theory (SCCT) Refining and Clarifying a Cognitive-Based Theory of Crisis Communication." *The Handbook of Crisis Communication*: 193–204.

Coombs, W. T and E.R. Tachkova. 2019. "Scansis as a Unique Crisis Type: Theoretical and Practical Implications." *Journal of Communication Management* 23(1): 72–88.

Coombs, W. T and Tachkova, E.R. 2024. "How Emotions Can Enhance Crisis Communication: Theorizing Around Moral Outrage." *Journal of Public Relations Research*: 1–17.

Carpenter, A and K. Greene. 2015. "Social Penetration Theory." *The International Encyclopedia of Interpersonal Communication* : 1–4.

Crisafis, A. Wave of Suicides at France Telecom. *The Guardian.* accessed January 11, 2024. http://tinyurl.com/revfyx6a.

Cropanzano, R., M.T. Dasborough and H.M.Weiss. 2017. "Affective Events and the Development of Leader-Member Exchange." *Academy of Management Review* 42(2): 233–258.

Disability: IN. September 2023 "Fast Company: Why Microsoft's Satya Nadella and Lowe's CEO Marvin Ellison Care About Disability Inclusion." *Disability: IN.* Accessed, December 29, 2023. http://tinyurl.com/wnf96ems.

Dobbin, F and A. Kalev. 2016. "Why Diversity Programs Fail." *Harvard Business Review* 94(7): 14.

Downey, S.N., L. van der Werff, K.M. Thomas and V.C. Plaut. 2015. "The Role of Diversity Practices and Inclusion in Promoting Trust and Employee Engagement," *Journal of Applied Social Psychology* 45(1): 35–44.

Drenten, J., R.L. Harrison and N.J. Pendarvis. 2023. "More Gamer, Less Girl: Gendered Boundaries, Tokenism, and the Cultural Persistence of Masculine dominance." *Journal of Consumer Research* 50(1), 2–24.

Eisenberg, E. M. 1984. "Ambiguity as Strategy in Organizational Communication." *Communication Monographs* 5(13), 227–242.

Feeley, J. September 28, 2023. "Johnson & Johnson Hit by 11,000 More Lawsuits Linking Baby Powder to Cancer After Judge Throws $9 Billion Settlement Case." *Fortune.* Accessed January 7, 2024. http://tinyurl.com/3pepkvxr.

Fenton, A., L. Gillooly and C.M. Vasilica. "Female Fans and Social Media: Micro-Communities and the Formation of Social Capital." 2023. *European Sport Management Quarterly* 23(2): 370–390.

Fernández-Ferrín, P., S. Castro-González and B. Bande. 2021 "Corporate Social Responsibility, Emotions, and Consumer Loyalty in the Food Retail Context: Exploring the Moderating Effect of Regional Identity." *Corporate Social Responsibility and Environmental Management* 28(2): 648–666.

Ferraro, C., H. Alicia and S. Sean. 2023. "Embracing Diversity, Equity, and Inclusion (DEI): Considerations and Opportunities for Brand Managers." *Business Horizons* 66(4): 463–479.

Gambeti, R. C., T. C. Melewar and D.M. Kelly D. 2017. "Guest Editors' Introduction: Ethical Management of Intangible Assets in Contemporary Organizations." *Business Ethics Quarterly* 27(3): 381–392.

Gates, D. March 15, 2019. "Flawed Analysis, Failed Oversight: How Boeing, FAA certified the Suspect 737 MAX Flight Control System." *The Seattle Times.* Accessed December 25, 2023. http://tinyurl.com/srna2exm.

Gates, D., M. Steve and K. Lewis. October, 2, 2019. "Boeing Rejected 737 MAX Safety Upgrades Before Fatal Crashes, Whistleblower says." *The Seattle Times.* Accessed December 25, 2023. http://tinyurl.com/pcv7fn2z.

Gavetti, G., H. Rebecca and G. Simona. 2005. *Kodak and the Digital Revolution (A).* Cambridge, MA: Harvard Business School Publishing.

General Motors. April 10, 2014. "GM Creates Speak Up For Safety Program For Employees. Two Engineers Placed on Leave as Part of Ignition Switch Probe." *General Motors Newsroom.* Accessed January 2, 2024. http://tinyurl.com/5ywthjxf.

Gershgorn, D. April 4, 2019. "Amid Employee Uproar, Microsoft is Investigating Sexual Harassment Claims Overlooked by HR." *Quartz.* Accessed December 28, 2023. https://rb.gy/kkqbbs.

Goh, S and M. Wasko. 2012. "The Effects of Leader-Member Exchange on Member Performance in Virtual World Teams." *Journal of the Association for Information Systems* 13(10): 1.

Greaves, T. 1994. *Intellectual property rights for indigenous peoples: A sourcebook.* Society for Applied Anthropology, PO Box 24083, Oklahoma City, OK 73124.

Grebe, S.K. 2013. "The Importance of Being Genuinely Sorry When Organizations Apologize: How the Australian Wheat Board (AWB Limited) was Damaged Even Further by Its Response to a Corporate Scandal." *Journal of Public Affairs* 13(1): 100–110.

Griffith, E. April 17, 2018. "19 Massive Corporate Social Media Horror Stories." *PC Mag.* Accessed on February 17, 2024. http://tinyurl.com/8y52hbk5.

Grunig, J.E and A.G. Larissa. 2013. "11 Models of Public Relations and Communication." *Excellence in public relations and communication management.*

Hastwell, C. July 14, 2022. The High Value of Building Pride in the Workplace. *Insights.* Accessed on January 10, 2024. http://tinyurl.com/4vfwu997.

Heinz History Center. "About the H.J. Heinz Company." http://tinyurl.com/2zfaymn2.

Hennig-Thurau, T., G.P. Kevin, G. Walsh and D.D. Gremler. 2004. "Electronic Word-of-Mouth Via Consumer-Opinion Platforms: What Motivates Consumers to Articulate Themselves on the Internet?" *Journal of interactive marketing* 18(1): 38–52.

Hydock, C., P. Neeru and T.J. Weber. 2019. "The Consumer Response to Corporate Political Advocacy: A Review and Future Directions." *Customer Needs and Solutions* 6: 76–83.

Hofstede, G. 2011. "Dimensionalizing Cultures: The Hofstede Model in Context." *Online Readings in Psychology and Culture* 2(1): 8.

Hong, C., and G.J. Yi. 2022. "When Transparent Leadership Communication Motivate Employee Advocacy: Testing the Mediator Roles of Employee Attributions in CEO Activism." *Public Relations Review* 48(3): 102202.

IBM. "Join the Call for Code Global Challenge." Accessed April 13, 2024. https://tinyurl.com/3rujun7s.

Isidore, C. December 10, 2015. "Death Toll for GM Ignition Switch: 124." *CNN.* Accessed September 30, 2023. https://tinyurl.com/mtsdxwh9.

Johnston, J., ed. 2020. *Public Relations: Theory and Practice.* Routledge.

Jordan, K. 2020. "Tales from the Real World: Employee Resource Groups (ERGs) as Advocates in Corporate America." In *Transformative Leadership in Action: Allyship, Advocacy & Activism*: 163–170. Emerald Publishing Limited.

Kent, M. L. 2015. "The Power of Storytelling in Public Relations: Introducing the 20 Master Plots." *Public Relations Review* 41(4): 480–489.

Kent, M.L and M. Taylor. 2002 "Toward a Dialogic Theory of Public Relations." *Public Relations Review* 28(1): 21–37.

Kent, M.L. 2023. "9 Dialogic Theory in Public Relations." *Public Relations Theory III: In the Age of Publics.*

Khan, O., N. Varaksina and A. Hinterhuber. 2024. "The Influence of Cultural Differences on Consumers' Willingness to Pay More for Sustainable Fashion." *Journal of Cleaner Production*: 141024.

Kidder, D. L., M.J. Lankau, D. Chrobot-Mason, K.A. Mollica and R.A. Friedman. 2004. "Backlash Toward Diversity Initiatives: Examining the Impact of Diversity Program Justification, Personal and Group Outcomes." *International Journal of Conflict Management* 15(1): 77–102.

Kim, D. J., M. Salvacion, M. Salehan and D.W. Kim. 2023. "An Empirical Study of Community Cohesiveness, Community Attachment, and their Roles in Virtual Community Participation." *European Journal of Information Systems* 32(3): 573–600.

Kim, H., Y. Hwang, J. Gim and Y. Cheng. 2024. "When are Vivid Hotel Photos Effective? The Moderating Effects of Resource Scarcity and Brand Level." *International Journal of Hospitality Management* 116: 103617.

Kluger, J. April 2, 2020. "To Fight COVID-19, Ford is Planning to Manufacture Ventilators. This isn't the First Time the Automaker has Made Medical Devices." *Time.* Accessed September 13, 2023. https://time.com/5814438/iron-lung-ventilator-ford/.

Kmia, O. December 14, 2022 "Why Kodak died and Fujifilm thrived: A Tale of Two Film Companies." *PetaPixel.* Accessed September 30, 2023. https://tinyurl.com/2kr5aw6t.

Kozinets, R.V. 2015. *Netnography: Redefined.* Sage, 2015.

Kwon, S and S. Ha. 2023. "Examining Identity- and Bond-Based Hashtag Community Identification: The Moderating Role of Self-Brand Connections." *Journal of Research in Interactive Marketing* 17(1): 78–93.

Lambert, C.A and C. Quintana. 2015. "Online Representations of Employee Resource Groups Inhibit Employee Engagement: A Critical/Cultural Analysis of Corporate Websites." *Prism* 12(2): 1–15.

Ledingham, J.A. 2006 "Relationship Management: A General Theory of Public Relations." *Public Relations Theory II*: 465–483.

Lee, C.T and S. Hsieh. 2022."Can Social Media-Based Brand Communities Build Brand Relationships? Examining the Effect of Community Engagement on Brand Love." *Behaviour & Information Technology* 41(6): 1270–1285.

Lee, J and L. Kwangho. 2023. "How Japanese Consumers Respond to Corporate Twitter Accounts: The Role of Perceived Personality and Parasocial Relationship." *Keio Communication Review* 34(45): 35–52.

Lee, Y and W. Tao. 2021. "Does Perceived Morality of CEO Activism Matter? Understanding Employees' Responses to CEO Actions on Sociopolitical Issues." *Management Decision* 59(10): 2329–2354.

Liao, Y., L. Bin, Z. Haiyan and Y. Xi. 2021. "The Power of Unrequited Love: The Parasocial Relationship, Trust, and Organizational Identification Between Middle-Level Managers and CEOs." *Frontiers in psychology* 12: 689511.

Lim, J.S and C. Young. 2021. "Effects of Issue Ownership, Perceived Fit, and Authenticity in Corporate Social Advocacy on Corporate Reputation." *Public Relations Review* 47(4): 102071.

Llamas, M. October 30, 2023. Talcum Powder Recall. *Drugwatch*. Accessed January 8, 2024. http://tinyurl.com/3rwttzw8.

Lloyd-Parkes, E., J.H. Deacon, A.J. Grant PhD, T. Simon. 2021. "Emotional Overload! A Dialogic Autoethnography of Scholar-Participant-Consumer Reactions to the Marketing of Thanatourism." *The Qualitative Report* 26(3): 992–1011.

Logan, N. 2021. "A Theory of Corporate Responsibility to Race (CRR): Communication and Racial Justice in Public Relations." *Journal of Public Relations Research* 33(1): 6–22.

Loi, R., K.W. Chan and L.W. Lam. 2014. "Leader–Member Exchange, Organizational Identification, and Job Satisfaction: A Social Identity Perspective." *Journal of Occupational and Organizational psychology* 87(1): 42–61.

Low, S., M. Poh, J. Bolong, M. Waheed and J. Wirza. 2022. "10-Year Systematic Literature Review of Social penetration in Online Communication."

Luu, H.N., L.H. Nguyen and J. Wilson. 2023. "Organizational Culture, Competition and Bank Loan Loss Provisioning." *The European Journal of Finance* 29(4): 393–418.

Maguire, M., and B. Delahunt. 2017. "Doing a Thematic Analysis: A Practical, Step-By-Step Guide for Learning and Teaching Scholars." *All Ireland Journal of Higher Education* 9(3).

Mahdy, F., M. Alqahtani and F. Binzafrah. 2023. "Imperatives, Nenefits, and Initiatives of Green Human Resource Management (GHRM): A Systematic Literature Review." *Sustainability* 15(6): 4866.

Maiorescu, R.D. 2016 "Crisis Management at General Motors and Toyota: An Analysis of Gender-Specific Communication and Media Coverage." *Public Relations Review* 42(4): 556–563.

Maiorescu-Murphy, R.D. 2019. *Corporate Diversity Communication Strategy*. Springer International Publishing.

Maiorescu-Murphy, R.D. 2021 "'We Are the Land:' An Analysis of Cultural Appropriation and Moral Outrage in Response to Christian Dior's Sauvage Scandal." *Public Relations Review* 47(4): 102058.

Maiorescu-Murphy, R.D. 2022. "Business-Centered Versus Socially Responsible Corporate Diversity Communication. An Assessment of Stakeholder (dis) Agreement on Twitter." *Public Relations Review* 48(1): 102138.

Maiorescu, R and B. Maryana. 2011. "Top Management Pressure That Leads to Suicide: A Critical Analysis of the France Telecome Suicide Crisis from the Perspective of the Linguistic Image Restoration Model." In *14TH INTERNATIONAL PUBLIC RELATIONS RESEARCH CONFERENCE*, 506.

Maiorescu, R and W. Brenda. 2016. *Diversity in Multinational Corporations.* Taylor & Francis.

Makhdoomi, U. and F. Nika. 2017 "Workforce Diversity and Employee Performance: An Empirical Study of Telecom Organizations." *Amity Global Business Review* 12, 107–115.

Mallory, D.B and D.E. Rupp. 2014. "Good Leadership: Using Corporate Social Responsibility to Enhance Leader-Member Exchange. *The Oxford Handbook of Leader Member Exchange,*" 1–20.

Mangus, S.M., D.E. Bock, E. Jones and J.A.G. Folse. 2020. "Examining the Effects of Mutual Information Sharing and Relationship Empathy: A Social Penetration Theory Perspective." *Journal of Business Research* 109: 375–384.

Martin, R., M. Ono, A. Legood, S.D. Dello and G. Thomas. 2023. "Leader–Member Exchange (LMX) Quality and Follower Well-Being: A Daily Diary Study." *Journal of Occupational Health Psychology* 28(2): 103.

Matei, S.A and R.J. Bruno. 2015. "Pareto's 80/20 Law and Social Differentiation: A Social Entropy Perspective." *Public Relations Review* 41(2): 178–186.

Matharu, G.K, T. von der Heidt, G. Sorwar and A. Sivapalan. 2024. "The Moderating Role of Hofstede's Cultural Dimensions on Consumer Purchasing of Organic food." *Journal of International Consumer Marketing* 36(1): 21–40.

McFadden, C. January 29, 2020. "7 Companies that Started Out in Someone's Garage." *Interesting Engineering.* Accessed December 27, 2023. http://tinyurl.com/3tjyh46e.

McGahan, A.M. 2023. "The New Stakeholder Theory on Organizational Purpose." *Strategy Science.*

McGregor, J. January 16, 2014. "Mary Barra: The Rare CEO Who Worked in Human Resources." *The Washington Post.* Accessed January 3, 2024. http://tinyurl.com/3jctbw9x.

Means, S.P. August 30, 2019. "Dior Pulls Johnny Depp's Filmed-in-Utah 'Sauvage' Ad After Complaints of Cultural Appropriation." *The Salt Lake Tribune.* Accessed May 8, 2024 https://tinyurl.com/y4xhk37h.

Meuser, J.D and J. Smallfield. 2023. "Servant leadership: The Missing Community Component." *Business Horizons* 66(2): 251–264.

Mekonnen, M and Z. Bayissa. 2023. "The Effect of Transformational and Transactional Leadership Styles on Organizational Readiness for Change Among Health Professionals." *SAGE Open Nursing* 9: 23779608231185923.

Microsoft. "Accessible Innovation. We Strive to Accelerate Innovation to Build a More Equitable and Accessible Future for Everyone." Accessed December 29, 2023. http://tinyurl.com/n5mfhcvd.

Min, J., K. Jiyoung and Y. Kiseol. "CSR Attributions and the Moderating Effect of Perceived CSR Fit on Consumer Trust, Identification, and Loyalty." *Journal of Retailing and Consumer Services* 72: 103274.

Moon, S., K. Seung-Wook and D. Iacobucci. 2023. "Dynamic Relationship Changes Between Reviewers and Consumers in Online Product Reviews." *Journal of Retailing.*

Mor Barak, M. E., G. Luria and K.C. Brimhall. 2022. "What Leaders Say Versus What they Do: Inclusive Leadership, Policy-Practice Decoupling, and The Anomaly of Climate for Inclusion." *Group & Organization Management* 47(4), 840–871.

Nadella, S. 2017. *Hit refresh.* Bentang Pustaka.

Nossiter, A. December 20, 2019. "3 French Executives Convicted in Suicides of 35 Workers." *The New York Times.* Accessed January 7, 2019. http://tinyurl.com/mre5jn68.

Okazaki, S., P. Kirk, W. Douglas and D.M. Héctor. 2020. "Exploring Digital Corporate Social Responsibility Communications on Twitter." *Journal of Business Research* 117: 675–682.

Olkkonen, L., and J. Jannica. 2019. "Corporate Activism: Exploring Corporate Social Responsibility (CSR) Communication." In *Academy of Management Proceedings,* (1): 17350. Briarcliff Manor, NY 10510: Academy of Management.

Our Ford Purpose. "We are Here for one Purpose, to Help Build a Better World, Where Very Person is Free to Move and Pursue their Dreams." *Ford Motor Company.* https://corporate.ford.com/microsites/our-purpose/index.html.

Pandolfo, C. January 30, 2024. "Toyota Chairman Issues Apology for Subsidiary Safety Scandal, Brand remains World's Top Seller." *Fox Business.* Accessed April 27, 2024. https://tinyurl.com/39ddxb97.

Park, J.Y and C. Kim. 2023. "The Role of Organizational Justice and Social Interaction in Mitigating the Negative Effects of High-Performance Member Retailers on Strategic Integration." *Journal of Retailing and Consumer Services* 72, 103238.

Patagonia 2024. "Clare Gallagher." Accessed April 13, 2024. https://tinyurl.com/3w4n96kb.

Perez, Chris. "Dior 'Sauvage' perfume ad campaign with Johnny Depp sparks outrage on social media." *Page Six.* August 30, 2019. https://tinyurl.com/yhd3tca4 (accessed May 8, 2024).

Pichierri, M and G. Pino. 2023. "Less Saturated, More Eco-Friendly: Color Saturation and Consumer Perception of Product Sustainability." *Psychology & Marketing* 40(9): 1830–1849.

Place, K.R. 2022. "Toward A Framework for Listening With Consideration for Intersectionality: Insights from Public Relations Professionals in Borderland Spaces." *Journal of Public Relations Research* 34(1–2): 4–19.

Polley, L. April 25, 2012. "Introducing the New Footprint Chronicles on Patagonia.com." *Patagonia.* Accessed April 13, 2024. https://tinyurl.com/5byshknz.

Pozzo, B. 2020. "Fashion Between Inspiration and Appropriation." *Laws* 9(1): 5.

Reed, B. March 22, 2022. Disney Workers Walk Out Over 'Don't Say Gay' Bill as Company Sends Mixed Messages. *The Guardian.* Accessed January 7, 2024 http://tinyurl.com/ncap45r2.

Sabuhari, R., A. Sudiro, D. Irawanto and M. Rahayu. 2020. "The Effects of Human Resource Flexibility, Employee Competency, Organizational Culture Adaptation and Job Satisfaction on Employee Performance." *Management Science Letters* 10(8):1775–1786.

Sagar Menghwar, P and F. Edward. 2023. *Stakeholder Theory.* SAGE Publications, Inc.

Schein, E.H. 2009. *The Corporate Culture Survival Guide* 158. John Wiley & Sons.

Schembri, S and L. Latimer. 2016. "Online Brand Communities: Constructing and Co-Constructing Brand Culture." *Journal of Marketing Management* 32(7–8): 628–651.

Scheyder, E. "Focus on Past Glory Kept Kodak from Digital Win." Reuters. Accessed September 30, 2023. https://tinyurl.com/y6mex89p.

Schwabenland, C and T. Frances. 2015. "Shadows and Light: Diversity Management as Phantasmagoria." *Human Relations* 68(12): 1913–1936.

Singh, N and S.K. Srivastava. 2011. "Impact of Colors on the Psychology of Marketing—A Comprehensive Overview." *Management and Labour Studies* 36(2): 199–209.

Sison, M.D. 2017. "Communicating Across, Within and Between, Cultures: Toward Inclusion and Social Change." *Public Relations Review* 43(1): 130–132.

Smith, Ruth C., and Eric M. Eisenberg. 1987. "Conflict at Disneyland: A Root-Metaphor Analysis." *Communications Monographs* 54(4): 367–380.

Society for Human Resource Management. October 17, 2023. "Employers Beware: Discrimination Lawsuits Continue to Rise." Accessed February 3, 2024. http://tinyurl.com/3rrx3da8.

Sommerfeldt, Erich J., and Aimei Yang. 2018. "Notes on a Dialogue: Twenty Years of Digital Dialogic Communication Research in Public Relations." *Journal of Public Relations Research* 30(3): 59–64.

Sriramesh, K. 2012. "Culture and Public Relations: Formulating the Relationship and its Relevance to the Practice." In *Culture and Public Relations*, 9–24. Routledge.

Stanford, S. September 13, 2023. "Henry Ford–An Impact Felt." *Henry Ford Heritage Foundation.* https://hfha.org/the-ford-story/henry-ford-an-impact-felt/.

Stojanović, A., M. Isidora, A. Sanela, U. Snežana and M. Ivan. 2020. "Corporate Social Responsibility as a Determinant of Employee Loyalty and Business Performance." *Journal of Competitiveness* 12(2): 149–166.

Sumarjo, W., H. Haerofiatna and H. Didit. 2024. "The Influence of Organizational Justice on Employee Performance Mediated Work Engagement." *Jurnal Mantik* 7(4): 3186–3193.

Sundheim, D. December 12, 2023. "How Patagonia Became the Most Reputable Brand in the United States." *Forbes.* Accessed April 13, 2024. https://tinyurl.com/3hcxbu95.

Tesla. "Elon Musk." Accessed December 23, 2023. http://tinyurl.com/4d2rba6h.

Theodorakopoulos, N and B. Pawan. 2015. "Guest Editors' Introduction: Diversity and Inclusion in Different Work Settings: Emerging Patterns, Challenges, and Research Agenda." *Human Resource Management* 54(2): 177–197.

Toeppe, J. February 4, 2023. "Ford vs. GM. A Tale of Two Auto Makers. Auto Expert: 'GM More Aligned Under Collaborative Leadership." *Fox Business.* Accessed January 3, 2024. http://tinyurl.com/523y7y6f.

Tourky, M., K. Philip and S. Ahmed Shaalan. 2020. "The Role of Corporate Identity in CSR Implementation: An Integrative Framework." *Journal of Business Research* 117: 694-706.

Valukas, R.A. 2014. "Report to Board of Directors of General Motors Company Regarding Ignition Switch Recalls." https://tinyurl.com/5n6ec3r4.

Vanhanen, S., M. Raunio, E. Heikkilä, and G. Olegário. 2023. "How Diversity Matters in Working Life: A Literature Review in a Finnish Context." *Migration Letters* 20(4): 76–87.

Varma, A, A. Jaiswal, V. Pereira and Y.L.N. Kumar. 2022. "Leader-Member Exchange in the Age of Remote Work." *Human Resource Development International* 25(2): 219–230.

Verčič, D and S. Krishnamurthy. 2019. "The Media, International, Transnational and Global Public Relations." In *The Global Public Relations Handbook*, 39–50. Routledge.

Wallington, C. 2024. *A Seat at the C-Suite Table: Insights from the Leadership Journeys of African American Executives.* Business Expert Press.

Wanta, W. 2023. *The Public and the National Agenda: How People Learn about Important Issues.* Taylor & Francis.

Windscheid, L., L. Bowes-Sperry J. Mazei and M. Morner. 2017. "The Paradox of Diversity Initiatives: When Organizational Needs Differ from Employee Preferences," *Journal of Business Ethics* 145(1): 33–48.

Wrench, J. 2005. "Diversity Management Can Be Bad for You." *Race & Class* 46(3): 73–84.

Yuan, S and L. Chen Lou. 2020. "How Social Media Influencers Foster Relationships With Followers: The Roles of Source Credibility and Fairness in Parasocial Relationship and Product Interest." *Journal of Interactive Advertising* 20(2): 133–147.

Zhan, M.M and Z. Xinyan. 2023 "Fostering Organization-Public Relationships Through Openness and Engagement: A Meta-Analysis." *Journal of Public Relations Research* 35(2): 86–112.

About the Author

Roxana D. Maiorescu is a Professor of Marketing Communication at Emerson College, Boston. She specializes in communication management and social media. She has conducted over 50 research projects that have appeared as journal articles, books, book chapters, and national/international conference proceedings. Her research has been published by Routledge, Palgrave Macmillan, Oxford University Press, Elsevier, and Sage.

Index

www.ingramcontent.com/pod-product-compliance
Lightning Source LLC
Jackson TN
JSHW011556070425
82147JS00008B/85